Kailash—M

Diary of a Pilgrim

This is a story of an unforgettable odyssey to the holy Mount Kailash and the sacred Lake Mansarovar describing mysteries connected with the land capturing the intangible air of faith and pilgrimage.

For four major religions of the world, i.e. for Tibetan Buddhism, Jainism, Bompo (a religion prior to Buddhism in Tibet) and Hinduism, Mount Kailash is the spot of utmost reverence and importance.

For the Buddhists, Kailash is the centre point of the universe. For the Jains, Kailash is the Mount Ashtapada and is a place of pilgrimage. For the Bompo followers, Kailash is the nine-faced Swastika Mountain and is constantly emanating great power. For the Hindus, Kailash is the Sumeru Parvat, the spiritual centre of the world around which all the earthly powers revolve.

If there are heavenly abodes on earth, Kailash-Mansarovar is to be treasured as one that is the most celestial.

Map of Kailash – Mansarovar
and
Gurla La

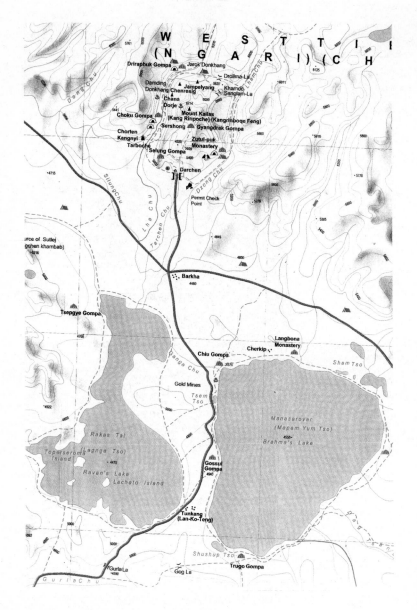

Kailash–Mansarovar

Diary of a Pilgrim

NILESH D. NATHWANI

New Age Books

ISBN: 81-7822-054-7

First Edition: 2002

Published by
NEW AGE BOOKS
A-44 Naraina Phase I
New Delhi-110 028 (INDIA)
Email: nab@vsnl.in
Website: www.newagebooksindia.com

Printed in India
at **Excel Printers**
C-206, Naraina Phase-I, New Delhi-110 028

DEDICATED
TO

LATE SRI KRISHNAPREM (RONALD NIXON)

WHOM I NEVER MET,

WHOSE BOOKS CONTINUE TO INSPIRE ME.

I WOULD LOVE TO BE LIKE

HIM.

ACKNOWLEDGEMENT AND
GRATITUDE TO

My Mother and Father. They love me. Had it not been for them I would not be. How would I have ever experienced the impact of Kailash-Mansarovar?

Amita, my wife, critic, friend and supporter who encouraged me to embark on this trip to Tibet.

Vinod Budhdeo who invited me on this adventure in the first instance.

Jagdish Trivedi, Kunj Trivedi, Dr. Hemant Mehta, Dr. (Mrs.) Mrinalini Mehta, Harish Kapadia and all who kept patience with me for five weeks.

I am grateful to Drs. Hemant and Mrinalini Mehta for making their exceptionally good photos available for this booklet. My profound gratitude to Jagdish Trivedi for providing statistics for this booklet and his suggestions.

Dipl. Ing. Prof. Walter Tschiedel for his excellent photo of Kailash in the night with stars.

Rajnikant J. Mehta and Gyanchandra of Arvind Chetna Samaj for their valuable help.

Geetika Sardana and Ilaben Budhdeo for reading this booklet in draft form and giving suggestions.

Ghandikota Ramesh for editing this booklet.

Pratibha Jobanputra who helped in the publication of this booklet. Her earnest effort to make this work flawless is highly appreciated.

Finally Niraj, Sonal and Suraj, my children, who inspired me to write this diary in detail that turned into this booklet.

I am immeasurably indebted to all these lovely people who nursed the birth of this booklet. Their roles have indeed left me bereft of all words. Taking a cue from Shakespeare, all I can say is *Thanks, thanks and thanks again even though good turns are often shuffled off with such uncurrent pay.*

Originally this letter, though in a far shorter version, was posted to my family and other friends from Kathmandu. It has still *retained* its original form. It is now addressed to all those who aspire to visit Kailash-Mansarovar.

NILESH D. NATHWANI

INTRODUCTION

On an October evening in 1999, at a marriage reception in London, I unexpectedly bumped into Kunj Trivedi, a friend from Kenya. I was surprised to meet him after so many years. More surprising than that was when he invited me to join him on an excursion to Tibet. The excursion was planned for April-May 2000, to take maximum advantage of good weather. The idea was to drive across Tibet to the holy mountain of Kailash and to the legendary lake Mansarovar where scores of spiritual men of India have acquired realisation. The offer was a tribute to me as much as an accredited accolade to a soldier. I am a born pilgrim. I call myself a pilgrim of this world since I love to see God in nature. Nature for me is the dynamic face of the Ultimate Reality that is immutable. Such adventures have constantly excited me and never would I let an opportunity like this be put aside. The group was to have a maximum of seven persons and would be led by an experienced mountaineer of Mumbai, Harish Kapadia. It is difficult to get Harish as a leader. He is as busy as a bee, travelling and leading numerous international mountaineers. Still, he agreed to lead these amateur trackers, as he is Kunj Trivedi's friend. Kunj himself is an avid photographer of a very high calibre. His 1998 calendar entitled CATS, won him international fame amongst photographers and friends. The calendar consists of the most brilliant photos of wildlife I have ever seen.

In this mission Kunj's aim was to take splendid photos of Kailash and Mansarovar. The expedition costs were high, though for this price utmost precision, panache and planning was offered. My 65 years of youth would also easily cope, Kunj assured me. I needed only to agree. This was almost a compliment to me and I agreed instantly. We needed one more companion. I straightaway thought of Nilesh Nathwani

X KAILASH-MANSAROVAR

in Vienna. Nilesh is not a very easy person to put up with. His thinking is different. He always comes up with new ideas at very odd moments, just as a magician pulls a rabbit out of the hat, unexpected. He has some plus points. He writes, takes nice photos and has a poetic eye to see, feel and describe nature. In his odd mood, he may decide to write a record of the yatra that he may publish, even when no one wants him to do so. He also sings, though never for a long time. His voice is neither a pleasure nor a pain to the ear. He has a macabre sense of humour. Yet he is kind, considerate and caring. So without hesitation I phoned him. I knew he would not dismiss the offer to be a part of this once in a lifetime venture. And I was right. Nilesh agreed without a second thought.

Now that the team was set, I set out to do my homework. Regular training at the local gym was imperative. This included half an hour of running on the track, half an hour of cycling and half an hour of bodybuilding. This went on until April 2000 with utmost discipline. At the same time the hunt to find all the available literature and maps on Kailash and Mansarovar continued. This occupied not just myself but the rest of the group, too. Disappointingly, not much literature was available. Bookshops did not offer much. Offers from Amazon.com were also not gratifying. We were looking for something from the Indian point of view, something that blended travel and philosophy. A lot of books were available on mountaineering and more than enough on Everest. Kailash and Mansarovar remained in obscurity. We got some information and photos from our group leader. Later on we found that the lack of literature and information was normal. While on our way back from Mansarovar we met a group of Indians - doctors and barristers - who were on their way to Kailash. They also lacked information. They asked us all sorts of questions. Whether we had seen some white swans swimming in Mansarovar or if the lake had lotus blooms. There is nothing like that at Mansarovar and yet there is much more. Mansarovar is half frozen even in summer and there are no inhabitants around the lake except for nomads on the move. There are neither temples nor pundits who offer to do your pujas. Still, not enough can be experienced or said.

The only way to submit information to such ardent seekers is to write our experiences. To tell these dedicated friends of Kailash and Mansarovar that we saw neither swans nor lotus nor met Gods who spoke to us. My fear was that if I asked Nilesh to release his diary to the public, he would not do so. So I kept my lips sealed. I have no idea what made him make public his experiences. This is a mystery for me as much as his person. However I am glad he decided to publish his story. I appreciate it and it is my pleasure to write this introduction to his *petite livre*.

This booklet is a living element of our gripping story of Mansarovar and Kailash. It is a tale about our fancies and fears, our adventures and aspirations, our expectations and disillusions, our escapes and retreats. It is a tale of our tents, our troubles and our treasures. And it is a tale of too remote cities. We travelled a long way to see them. The route we travelled was full of hardship. Hence, if any of you visiting Kailash and Mansarovar benefits from our experiences, our purpose is served. In a few years from now a motorway to Kailash and Mansarovar will surely be constructed and change the yatra. That will be the beginning of a new culture of pilgrimage in Tibet. One can then imagine *dhabas* (wayside food stalls), restaurants and hotels along the motorway. Kailash-Mansarovar may become so much of a tourist attraction that future visitors may witness the Gods in more luxury than that offered in heaven. Filmmakers may also discover and commercialise this paradise. Our tale will then have little merit. That is perhaps the future scenario. For the present, some individuals may possibly profit from this diary. Some other aged persons, who have kindled a lifetime desire to make a journey to Kailash-Mansarovar before their *final journey* and who are physically unable to do so now, may read this booklet, live our pilgrimage and bless us. For us there can be no bigger blessings.

22 Raisins Hill, Pinner   VINOD BUDHDEO
Middlesex, U.K.
26th October 2000

CONTENTS

LIST OF ILLUSTRATIONS

Diary

Route Map

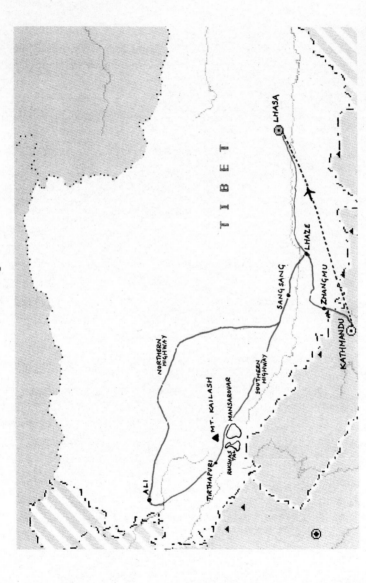

Mansarovar, Tibet
13 April - 17 May 2000

Dear friends,

I send my greetings from the East. Here are a few pages of my diary.

On 13 April 2000, I arrive at Kathmandu Tribhuvan airport and am garlanded by Raju, our travel agent. *Tribhuvan* literally means three worlds, I feel as if I am going to enter a journey to the three worlds of esoteric planes. I have travelled much in my life. This time I have completely different intentions. The difference lies in my attitude. In the past I travelled for a holiday or distraction. This time I am travelling for fulfilment. Hence this is a journey with a lot of emotions.

At Kathmandu we stay at the Hotel Vaishali, which offers a lot of luxuries. On 14 April we walk through the city to get our first impressions. Kathmandu impresses me with its historical Durbar Square and Pashupatinath Temple. Looking at the idol of Pashupatinath carved on a black stone (probably a meteor) one feels that He has a mystic power. I think the eyes are living and watching me intensely. It reminds me of a few lines of an eloquent sonnet called *The Stone Goddess:*

> *In a town of gods, housed in a little shrine,*
> *From sculptured limbs the Godhead looked at me,-*
> *A living Presence deathless and divine,*
> *A Form that harboured all infinity.*

SRI AUROBINDO

The temple's architecture is splendid; all the kings of Nepal have donated liberally to its construction. In this way they intended to gratify the deity Pashupatinath, the protector of animals and living beings. The kings may have won His favour and found a very palatial place in the Higher World. However, I wish one could confirm such a notion. All knowledge is not at our disposal in this life. Vinodbhai and myself walk in the Lord's domain and also perform a puja in hopes of gaining the special treatment of the Lord. We offer Him flowers and fruits:

पत्रं पुष्पं फलं तोयं यो मे भक्त्या प्रयच्छति ।
तदहं भक्त्युपहृतमश्नामि प्रयतात्मनः   ।।

भगवत् गीता, ९:२६ ।।

Pattram pushpam phalam toyam,
Yo me bhaktyā Prayacchati,
Tad aham bhaktyupahrtam,
Asnāmi prayatatmanah.

Fruits, water, flowers or leaves,
That in worship one offers me,
In delight My heart receives,
Lovingly blessing my devotee.

(BHAGWAT GITA, 9:26)

We try to please Him with our devotion. The temple is in the eastern end of the town where the two rivers Bagmati and Vishnumati flow. The banks of these rivers have an unusual, haunting atmosphere - it is the town's crematorium! We walk there, take photos and watch the monkeys who live there and are protected by the deity. At one point a monkey snatches a plastic bag of sugared groundnuts from my hand and shares the bounty with his friends. I do not fret. It is an abrupt and surprising attack on me. Rather amused by the attack, I stare at the monkey. He looks in my eyes with no guilt. A sadhu watching this scenario comes to me and says, *your offering to the Gods has been sincere.*

The Protector Himself has accepted the offering through the monkey. His words please Vinodbhai and myself immensely.

On 15 April we travel to a remote village in Nepal. We spend the 15th and 16th in a holiday resort called *Nagarkot* in complete tranquillity. Here our team is complete when Jagdishbhai arrives from Hong Kong to join us. Nagarkot is an hour's drive from Kathmandu on a dusty and winding uphill road. If the visibility is crystal clear, which is rare, one can have a distant view of Everest. Nagarkot is also known for its stimulating sunsets. The idea of spending two days in Nagarkot is to acclimatise and prepare us for the long journey in mountainous Tibet. We go for long walks and enjoy the mountain air, relaxing in the tranquil ambience of nature in Nepal. No one should attempt a pilgrimage to Tibet without acclimatisation. This golden rule should be observed to obtain the ultimate joy of travelling. To be sick and to travel is a curse. On the 17th, we return to Kathmandu to prepare ourselves for the flight to Lhasa, the next stage of our pilgrimage.

Today is 18 April. It is a full moon night. Kailash will be in full glory. It is an auspicious day dedicated to Lord Shiva. It is an excellent day to start a journey - a journey to Kailash. We fly to Lhasa. A realisation of a dream is in the making. On the plane a Lama is flying with us. He is flying with a group of his followers. Ten minutes after taking off, we see the Himalayan range. An ocean of mountains stretches below us. It is a sight of wonder. The immense impact it leaves on my mind tells me that this is the proof that a mighty power, who we call God, exists. There is no need for an ontological argument to prove His existence. Beauty is one of the rare things that lead to the proof that God exists.

No one is blinder than one who does not want to see Him in His creation. The beauty of the Himalayan world captivates our souls. First we see Gaurishankar and Kanchenjunga, a set of very beautiful mountains. Harishbhai points out Everest. Everest's indigenous name is *Sagarmath*, meaning the cliff in the ocean of mountains (how poetic). Below us is the Sagarmath in full stretch, in the true meaning of the word. Adjacent to Sagarmath is Makalu, an unusual peak standing majestically. We continue to be wonderstruck. We are so deeply engrossed in the Himalayas beneath us. Time turns to a moment. The flight is short. We do not realise that we are flying in the Tibetan sky.

Soon Lhasa is sighted. We try to have a bird's eye view of the Potala Palace. I can't see it. We descend. Gonggar airport has a strange atmosphere. It is fully guarded for security and one really feels that big brother is watching constantly. The Lama flying with us gets a flamboyant welcome. A large number of Buddhist priests in saffron coloured robes receive him. Each one is presented with a silk scarf from the Lama as blessing. I also feel as if I am a part of the Lama sect. Jigme, our Tibetan guide receives us by putting a silk scarf on us as well. The airport is ninety-six kilometres away from the centre of the city and it is one and a half hour's drive to Lhasa.

The ride to Lhasa is beautiful along the river Brahmaputra. Entering Lhasa, we are surprised to see that it is a modern city with numerous hotels and a shopping arcade. My eyes look for Potala Palace. Not in sight as yet. I have to wait until the evening. The first time I see it is in the shadow of dusk. On 19, 20 and 21 April, we see and are able to photograph Potala to our heart's contents. The Potala palace got its name from the hill on which it stands, the Potala meaning the *Red Mountain*. Lhasa is 3660 metres above sea level and is called the roof of the world. It is surrounded by dark and barren hills. The river Skyid Chu that is a tributary of the Brahmaputra flows on the side of the city.

After the Chinese occupation of Tibet, in October 1950 and in the absence of the Dalai Lama, the cultural heritage of the city has been slowly diminishing. The flight of the Dalai Lama to India led to the closing of many monasteries followed by insane killings. The occupation brought constant

The Potala Palace
(Photo by the author)

denigration of Tibetan religious practices. Monasteries and temples were pulled down and no religious rites were allowed even in the event of death. The conqueror dictated terms and influences. The national museum in the city still imposingly voices the Chinese influence on the culture of Tibet. Its sole purpose is to justify the occupation. However, one cannot fail to see the massive Indian influence.

Modernisation and development are acceptable, but not at the cost of an ancient heritage. One cannot deny the fact that Lhasa, as all other cities of the world, needs to modernise. During the Cultural Revolution in the 1960s life for the monks deteriorated distinctly until the government reversed its policy on religion. After the Cultural Revolution, China reversed its policies by restoring the Tibetan culture. Religious freedom is now largely restored, monasteries are allowed to be reopened and rebuilt. Traditional rites and practices are again permitted. Once again one can smell the fragrant incense in the air, pray with rosaries and turn prayer wheels in the monasteries. Lhasa is recently modernised and is a city of greater opulence and beauty than Kathmandu simply by virtue of its altitude and history. While Kathmandu is polluted, Lhasa is dirt-free, cold, sunny and submerged totally in its historical cultural beauty. The Chinese have recently understood that the loss of Tibetan cultural heritage would stagnate the economic growth of Tibet. Hence they have revitalised it by maintaining the culture of Tibet.

The Potala, with its immense treasures of gold, art and architecture is now maintained for tourists and brings admiration for the Chinese administration. It is a big source of income. The numerous large palace rooms are full of scroll paintings - metal and wooden images decorated in rich gold. These images display a culture based purely on religion. The paintings show ancient legendary tales, historic events, the behaviour, attitude and minute gestures of deities and demons. The deities and the demons are characterised through varying colour tones and different facial expressions. The deities display peaceful, poised and moderate expressions, while the demons show expressions of anger and destruction. There are several rooms with tombs of deceased Lamas. These rooms have massive gold figures of lions and display the wealth of the Tibetan rulers of the past. Yak butter lamps burn constantly around domes and devout Tibetans pray and meditate in silence. One can enter these meditation enclaves with shoes on. I feel very happy to see the grandeur of Tibet, displayed abundantly in the rooms of the splendid Potala Palace. One certainly gets the general impression that the Potala is very rich and well maintained. There is not much corruption. I enjoy the time spent at the palace very much.

I am very conscious that the ground of Potala is where my great hero, Nagarjun, once walked. I feel I have to say a little about this great hero. Nagarjun's life is very interesting. Nagarjun, Hindu turned Buddhist philosopher, magician-alchemist, is the founder of the Middle Path (*Madhyamika*) of Mahayana Buddhism. Records verify that Nagarjun was born about 800 years after Buddha, probably in southern India and was of a Brahmin-priestly-family. From his childhood one and only one idea obsessed him - how to make gold out of iron. He was an infant prodigy *par excellence*. In his childhood he learnt chemistry, physics and the science of metals. Later, in search of gold, he turned to inner disciplines to invoke inner powers. His ardent search for inner latent powers probably took him to Tibet. He turned towards inner disciplines of Buddhism. In this way he ended up by living in what I would call the *Goldmine of Nirvana*. He was one of the greatest scholars that lived in the tide of times. Two of his famous books clearly present his most scholarly views: the *Mula-Madhyamika Karikas* (Fundamentals of the Middle Way) and the *Vigrahavyavartani* (Treatise on Averting). He summarised that the perfection of wisdom ends with spiritual realisation of the transitory phenomenal world. His teaching has found a great echo amongst the monks living

around the Potala. The Potala air is full of this recognition.
Nagarjun lived in Lhasa. His footsteps marked on his beloved metal gold are still worshipped here at the Potala
Palace. We are guided to these footsteps just by chance. A
high-ranking Lama, coming to know that we are Indians,
gives us great honour and respect. He welcomes us with
dignity and we request him for a group photo with him.
After the photo, he takes us to a small chamber where
Buddhist spiritual seniors meditate. He takes us to the
footsteps of Nagarjun. I bow down to the footsteps reveren-
tially. For me it is a heart touching moment of reverence.
This moment of my life is very precious and shall never
be forgotten. Potala Palace reminds me of Nagarjun every
moment.

After that we reach the highest elevation of the Palace. We
come to the big terrace of the palace that overlooks the city.
It is a large terrace with rooms in the middle. The rooms
look like the *barsati* (terrace rooms) of the Indian houses.
The architectural influence of Bhutan or Ladakh is very
evident. From the top of the palace, one can see that the city
of Lhasa still has its ancient fragrance in the air. Buried in its
surrounding hills, it has mystical air that floats in the atmosphere. The slanting sunrays cloak the immediate plains with
a beautiful yellow-orange rust hue. From the terrace one can
see the Stupa of the Drepung Monastery, which is like the
Mandala (crown) of Indian temples. On the terrace we meet
a number of high ranking Chinese military officers. They are
escorting two Chinese film actresses. Beautiful small crea-
tures, well dressed in designer costumes, they wear constant,
serene smiles on their faces, as if fishing for compliments.
Both the actresses have artists' flair and fragrance. We have
a series of photographs with them. They are kind to us and
we are polite to them. One member of our party dubs this
gesture as *flirting* and warns that it can have grave negative
consequences on the Tibetan group of our party. The Chinese officers may harass Jigme, our local guide. This, I think

On the Roof of the Potala Palace
(Photo by the author)

is an irrational fear. I refuse to be threatened with fear. Times
have changed, as has the conservative view. Though the
invaders of Tibet are communists they are still open to the
new trend in politics. There is a new trend in communism.
That was of course not possible in the olden times.

Modern Lhasa is completely different from Nagarjun's. We
also visit the Nebulinka (also known as Napulinka) meaning
the Jewel Palace. While the Potala is the winter palace of the
Dalai Lama, the Nebulinka is his summer palace. We visit the
rooms where the Dalai Lama learned English, politics and
modern science from his Austrian tutor Heinrich Harrar who
lived almost seven years in Tibet after the Second World
War. The Dalai Lama's immense interest in science and
communication technology is evident when we hear that
once as a child, he opened and reassembled a radio that
brought him news from all over the world. The radio is still
kept in his room. The Dalai Lama is also very fond of flowers
and greenery. His summer palace has a beautiful garden.
The garden has weeping willows, junipers and elm trees.
There are also fruit trees such as peach, walnut, apple, pear
and apricot. As it is springtime, the fruit trees are not in
bloom as yet. The entrance of the palace has flower plants
of rose, marigold, carnation and gladiolus bearing a few
buds at this time of the year. The palace also has a library
where ancient manuscripts are preserved. The archives include
some manuscripts of Nagarjun's treatises. The Dalai Lama's
ambience is felt in the palace despite his physical absence.
I am very thankful to His Holy Highness for all that is offered
at the palace. I hope to send him this diary at his Dharamsala
address.

Lhasa has an opera house too, though a small one. Our
travel agent has planned an opera for us on the 21st.
However on a short notice it has been cancelled, as the
opera artists have to entertain the Chinese military delegation.
This sort of sudden change in programme for the government
officials surprises us all. This is the typical communist way of

Grand Buddha at Tashilumpu Monastery
(Photo by Dr. Hemant Mehta, FRPS)

leadership. Still, Lhasa fascinates me. Lhasa has an ancient monastic school devoted to the teaching of medicine, which we could not visit.

On 20 April we visit the famous Jokang Monastery, a very important monastery of Tibet. This is our first visit to a monastery in Tibet. It has an unusual, esoteric ambience. The fidelity to rituals performed by the local Tibetans can be seen in the eyes of the devotees. With postures of absolute dedication and devotion, prayer wheels in hands, the devotees chant mantras and invoke Buddha. From the balcony of the monastery, through the smoke of the incense, one can see the magnificent Potala in full glory as it stands on the red hill. On the roof of the monastery is the eye-catching Wheel of Dharma (right conduct) symbolising Buddha's historic sermon on Dharma. We take a lot of photographs. We have lunch at an Indian restaurant. Lhasa has modern restaurants, plenty of cyber *cafés*. We have our supper at the Tibetan restaurant and see the local opera that was called off the previous day. Opera in Lhasa is an unusual experience.

On 22 April we visit the Sera Monastery, one of the largest monasteries situated in the mountains, five kilometres north of Lhasa. The monks wear yellow caps and at one time more than five thousand monks lived at the monastery. Now there are only a few hundred monks. There is a large meditation hall and monks study, discuss and debate on the scriptures of Buddhism. The western term monk is slightly misleading if used for Buddhists monks as its equivalent in Tibetans *trapa* means scholar or a student of spirituality. I try and talk to a few monks to understand the rules of the monastery. We also visit the Drepung Monastery, at one time the largest monastery in Tibet and one of the largest in the world. It is an unforgettable experience.

Lhasa will ever remain alive in my memory especially for the Potala, Sera and Drepung monasteries. This is despite the fact that I have constant headaches in the evenings and feel a little feverish. A regular dose of Arsenic Alb^{200}D

Group Photograph: From left to right: Harish Kapadia, Kunj Trivedi, the Author, Jagdish Trivedi, Vinod Budhdeo and Dr. Mrinalini Mehta
(Photo by Dr. Hemant Mehta, FRPS)

(homeopathy medicine) helps me immensely in curing the headaches due to the high altitude. At an altitude of 3660 metres, it is a known medical fact that only half of the required oxygen molecules enter our lungs. The effect is shortness of breath and headache. One should drink as much as three times the volume of liquid one normally drinks. I force that much liquid down my throat. Still the altitude has already affected me.

On 23 April, Sunday, we drive towards Gyantse, south-west from Lhasa, crossing the famous Brahmaputra River. We have two Toyota Landcruisers and one truck. The truck carries our tents, petrol for the entire trip and our ration for the next four weeks. We are a group of fourteen people. Jagdishbhai is from Hong Kong. Kunjbhai is from Mumbai, Hemantbhai and Mrinalben are from Wales, Vinodbhai is from London, Harishbhai, our expedition leader, the famous Indian mountaineer and author of eight books, is from Mumbai. I am from Vienna. Jigme is Tibetan and our senior guide. Dorje, a Gurkha and veteran mountaineer, is the chief of Nepalese staff travelling with us. Dawa and Motilal are cooks who have trained themselves to cook Indian, Chinese and continental dishes. We are an excellent group and are determined to have tasty wholesome food during our drive through Tibet. We also have three very good drivers: Dawa, Lee and Pasang La.

Over the past decade the Chinese government has built a northern highway with crude stones. We are going to drive on this highway. In the early morning we leave Lhasa after a short prayer. The sun shines. Our hearts are full of hope and soaring spirits. As we set off, I feel like a painter in front of an empty canvas. Tibet - beautiful, immense, timeless, unending starched out before me is filled with mystery, bearing a million different expressions. I feel curious and anxious. The road before me winds round distant hills. Huge white clouds hang in the transparent blue of the sky. It is a memorable drive through grasslands broken by twisting mountain ridges and valleys dotted with bright sapphire blue salt lakes. At one lake we stop for a while. The lake is very interesting in shape. The water has sapphire blue colour mixed with white foam on top of the waves. There is an atmosphere of magic as the waves heave and break with spray and sparkle in the sunshine. This is an extremely beautiful spectacle for me as I watch and try to meditate. There appears to be some memory of it in my subconscious. In Lhasa, in a dream state, in the middle of a mystical experience, I saw myself at a very beautiful lake. The road through which I strolled to reach the lake was of a strange kind, never seen before. In the dream, I remember, it was deserted. The word lagoon came to my mind. This place is the same as the one in the dream. There is no one around. This lake, I realise, is the lagoon of my dream. As we continue our journey, at dusk we pass by another salt lake. I witness a grandiose sunset. The twilight that is disappearing but wants to survive shows its splendour. The display is splendid and amazingly impressive. It is a sky, I have never seen before. No words can describe what the eyes behold.

After witnessing this unusually picturesque landscape, we arrive at Gyantse in the evening hours. We stay at a Chinese hotel. At Gyantse there is an Anti-British Imperialists Museum, which we visit the next morning. It is a very interesting account of British invasion of 1904 under the leadership of General Francis Younghusband. The Tibetans could not defeat this invasion. It is fascinating to note how the present rulers manipulate history. The British are portrayed as demons attempting to win an inalienable part of Tibet. Old photographs are displayed in one room to support their side of the history. The most significant story of Younghusband is that, on the eve of his departure from Lhasa, the general experienced a wave of spiritual peace descending over him, which changed his life completely, and he became a vociferous voice of religion that founded the World Congress of Faiths in 1936. This was the same platform where Swami Vivekanand also spoke.

In the afternoon we visit the famous Gyantse Kumbum
Chorten; an amazing temple with several carved and painted
statues of Buddha. The Chorten rises over several floors and
is surmounted by a golden dome overlooking the landscape
of Gyantse. One can climb upwards for six stories and see
the grandeur of the Buddhist artists. All levels of the temple
till the high cupola excite a feeling of wonder. It is a long
day for us. So after an early Tibetan dinner that includes
haldi (turmeric) potatoes marinated with lots of Tibetan
basil, we are ready to rest. After a short discussion of Indian
politics and Tibetan tantric practices, we all go to sleep.

It is 24 April. The night's rest does me good. I am ready
for a drive to Shigatse, the second largest town in Tibet.
Today we are to visit Tashilumpu Monastery. This is the seat
of Panchan Lama, who is 13 years young. In the monastery,
a copper statue of grand Buddha that is 37 metres tall is
highly impressive. The statue contains nearly three hundred
kilos of gold. Pearls and precious stones are abundantly
used in the decoration of the statue. Buddha lives here - this
feeling is omnipresent. Hence Vinodbhai and I go around
this mega Buddha statue. Another statue of Buddha with
tears in His eyes (for the damage done in the name of the
Cultural Revolution) is interesting. The mind refuses to
accept the tears clearly seen on the face of Buddha.

Faith dominates. I remember my ideal, the Englishman
Ronald Nixon (adopted name Krishnaprem). During the pre-
independence days of India, Sri Aurobindo once said about
him, *here is a mind that can not only think but also see, look
into the core.* I rank him as one of the great rational minds
on the Indian academic scene of that time. His books and
particularly his letters, published now, sparkle with brilliant
flashes of high intelligence and deep spirituality. Whenever
I read his writings, I get a feeling that these were specially
written for me, to quench my thirst for esoteric enquiry. I
never met him. I regret it very much. He is no more.
Harishbhai, our mountain specialist and tour leader, met him

once, this he tells me. The English literary society has kept very quiet on the writings of Krishnaprem, as he has written only on Indian spirituality and mysticism. I sincerely feel that some day his very valuable contribution to literature will be recognised by the world. He was a professor at Lucknow University. It is not easy to transform a highly developed, rational mind into unconditional devotion. He practiced yoga and succeeded in transforming his highly rational mind. Krishnaprem is a living paragon of prem-bhakti or devotion though he is not the only one.

Bhakti is a very suitable instrument to unite and identify with God. Thinking of great Krishnaprem, and deep in our devotion, we chant the 'Om mani padme hum' (Hail to the Jewel in the Lotus) Mantra and go around the grand statue of Buddha. Since our arrival in Kathmandu, Vinodbhai and myself regularly hold a joint session of prayers. At times I pray with Jagdishbhai who magically chants the mantras in his tenor voice. Mrinalini joins us every time. We have not only prayers and meditation but also a lot of fun. One incident I have to narrate. Vinodbhai and I go to the market to buy some fruits. Vinodbhai is keen on carrying out a prank. He buys a Lama's costume, red robes and a red cape. He wears the costume and we come back to the hotel. The people there think he is a real Lama. The local Tibetans bow down to him for blessings. The Chinese soldiers look puzzled. Vinodbhai looks different. The hotel reception does not recognise him. His looks are very much transformed in this costume. The costume suits him so much. Tall as he is, with little or no hair on his head, his forehead shining and his eyes focused in the distance as if on Eternity, even I feel like bowing down to him. I make a genuine posture to him as if pleading for his blessings. He grants it with great grace. Our group finds this incident hilarious. After a good laugh we go to sleep.

Today is 25 April and we drive on to Lhatse on the Northern Highway. The drive is long and I am not well. The landscape is beautiful but I keep dozing off. After a long drive of about 220 kilometres we camp for the first time. Dorje and his assistants pitch our tents. We tent in the middle of a wide plateau surrounded by distant hills. Our Tibetan guide Jigme tells me that in winter this plateau is extraordinarily cold, with deadly blizzards and volatile snow-storms. Temperatures can drop 30 degrees in a single day as unexpected and ferocious winds usher in powerful and horrible hailstorms. We realise that our tents are old fashioned. Living in an **A** shaped tent is rather difficult. In a two metre by two metre tent there is very little place for two persons to move around. The tent is only one and a half metres high at the apex and very uncomfortable.

Vinodbhai is tall and he finds it very difficult to stand erect or dress in the tent. We wish that our travel agent had provided us with better tents that are inverted **U** shaped and more comfortable. After all we have paid so much to the travel agent. I have fever and I find it difficult to sleep. The night is long, cold, windy and most difficult. It snows and it is freezing in the night. The thermometer is showing $-7°C$. With the cold winds the wind chill has an effect of $-17°C$. While lying down I inevitably doze off with my arm touch-ing the tent. My arm is frozen and numb next morning. The tent is leaking. What luck! We are approximately 5000 metres high. I feel progressively worse. Vinodbhai gives me anti-biotics. If you look at the map we are north of Mount Everest.

On the 26 April we drive still westwards to Sangsang. I am feeling better. The antibiotics have worked. It is torturous to sit in a car that bumps every minute. The roads are full of potholes. At times the roads are wet with the wild, small water streams flowing from God knows where. At such places the roads are seamed with ruts. On such roads driving is no fun. At one stage the truck with our tents and rations gets stuck on a muddy patch. With one jeep we try to pull the bogged truck out by tying a rope and pulling from front. At the same time the other jeep pushes the truck from the back, bumper-to-bumper. The truck is heavily loaded. With every turn of the wheel the truck sinks deeper in the soft, soggy and sticky mud. Dawa takes the steering of the truck in his hands, hits the gas gently but with jerks until the truck rolls out. Once the wheels roll out from the sinking mud, he hits the gas hard and drives out on the hard stone road. Lee, his colleague Dawa and the truck driver Pasang La display super driving techniques and we get out of the mess.

Before dusk, we camp at a very remote place between the hills wide away from Sangsang. It is a dry and arid landscape of forbidding grandeur and infinite horizons. The evening is bright, with a blue sky, reddish-orange clouds and winds with freezing temperatures. The plateau is surrounded by small hills and there are neither trees nor shrubs. There are no birds or animals to be seen in the vicinity. The desolate area is uninhabited or only sparsely populated. We meet no nomads. We are at a height of about 5000 metres. We have a long walk on a rocky and dry valley.

Vinodbhai thinks there is a lone lion in the vicinity. I wonder if there are any lions about. Never heard of them in Tibet. When we return to our tent, we watch the carnivorous animal closer with a pair of binoculars. It turns out to be a huge, solo mountain fox looking for leftovers. Our fears disappear. After the walk, our kitchen personnel serve us with Bombay *Bhelpuri*. In the evening our supper consists of Madras *Dosa*. It begins to cool further before it starts getting dark. Winds rage ruthlessly and there is nothing to break their accelerating power. Then comes the enveloping darkness, not at all the sort you see at dusk. Something similar to a blue haze that is desperate to swallow the daylight. It is not the black of the night but the dimmest of light that prevails. I retire. I am not well and my appetite is gone. I have lost the sense of taste. Breathing is getting more difficult. Meditating is also a hard effort. I am unable to sleep. Peeping out of my tent in the sky that has turned darker, I see a shooting star. My mother had once told me that if one were able to make an instant wish while the shooting star is still visible, one's wish would be fulfilled. I spontaneously wish for *the vision of Shiva*. This sudden wish surprises me. It is evident that this must have been dominating my subconscious all the while.

On 27 April, we drive towards Sangsang. The drive is long and picturesque while it cuts through lovely hills. We have a short lunch break at Rag. We continue driving, covering more than 200 kilometres on the stony remote road. We decide to pitch at Gayser hot springs vicinity. The sulphur hot springs are enlisted in the World Heritage List and the area is a centre of research in energy development. A group of Chinese scientists live here to study the springs that spurt as high as 30 metres. They watch and experiment with the nature. It is an excellent site to take photos, though springs offer no possibility to take a sulphur bath, as the water is not tapped and is dangerous to approach. The springs are kept natural, wild and are not meant to attract tourists as yet. The night of the 27th is warmer with the discomfort of living in the tent rapidly increasing.

On the morning of 28 April, we pass by Lake Daggyai that is not far from the Gayser hot springs. It is a most unusual site to photograph. The shores give contours of ice in the formation of waves. The effect is that of a sculpture on display whose outstanding figures are on frozen water. At the centre of the lake the water reflects a deep blue never seen before in my life. We spend quite some time and Kunjbhai and Hemantbhai go far to the shore to capture unique frames. As we have spent more time at Lake Daggyai, we make no more stops. Our next stop is at the Donco pass. We continue driving until the sunset. At dusk we arrive at a small town called Gerze. We decide not to pitch. We stay at the local Chinese guesthouse. I am not in favour of pitching a tent and everyone else in the group agrees in unison for obvious reasons. The local guesthouse provides no luxury but at least a room where we can stand erect. Huge warm

The Little One
(Photo by the author)

water thermos flasks and teabags are provided. Mostly a room consists of four beds. The prices are negligible for us coming from the West.

On 29 April, we start comfortably at about 10 a.m. for our next destination Gegyie. The roads are dry, stony and uncomfortable as the car bumps constantly. It is a drive in the wilderness. There is nothing worth visiting on the way. There are no monasteries or historical sites that can hold us. It is a monotonous, endless drive as we look at hills on both sides. Despite my ardent efforts to keep my eyes open, I constantly doze off only to be woken by bumps followed by bangs on the roof of the car. We spent the night at Gegyie, again in a local guesthouse. On 30th morning we start our long drive to Ali in the wilderness.

On 1 May, past midnight, we arrive at a city called Ali, also known as Shiquane. The drive is long. We are on the road for 14 hours and the drivers take the risk of travelling through the late night. I have no idea what we can do in case of a breakdown. We reach Ali past midnight. Our Chinese hotel is as dark as a dungeon. We manage to pull the hotelkeeper out of her bed. She switches on the main light from her room that lights all the rooms of the hotel. After she allocates rooms, she forgets to switch it off so we end up sleeping with lights on as there is no way to switch them off and return to darkness. There is also no place one can complain or even profess gratitude. The rooms have attached bathrooms and toilets but all broken and in a real mess. Sitting long hours in cars have cramped our muscles. Our limbs are aching. We sleep without complaining.

The next day we locate a public shower in the main street and have our first shower after days. A Chinese policewoman escorts us through the town that is a very important military strategic point for the Chinese occupation of Tibet. From here the Ladakh-Tibet borders are constantly guarded and a lot of military movement is seen. It is also a crossroads of business. From time immemorial many great personalities have visited this place as it is situated at the bank of the River Indus. There is a long shopping avenue with hills on both the ends. One of the hills is a military base camp and hence it is forbidden to climb. We climb the second hill and view the vast stretching plain between Tibet and Ladakh, India. A busy road to Aksai Chin lying amidst a background of the Himachal Pradesh peaks is a sight that can be best described as *a photographer's paradise*. On the other side, the River Indus flows by the side of the hill as if a silver ribbon is unwinding.

The hill is a showcase of the Tibetan culture. Lovely shining stones bear writings of holy texts. The Tibetan script is derived from Devanagari. It clearly shows the Indian influence on the local culture. Memory stones of the departed family members, and relics of beloved animals are seen everywhere. Flags of diverse colours and sometimes even the clothes for the departed souls are seen as we walk downhill. On the street some young boys follow me. They want to communicate with me. I speak to them in English. They also manage to convey their messages through broken English. They are impressed with their own skills of the language. I give them some toffees and ballpoint pens. They offer to take me shopping. I go to a small shop and buy some fountain pens for my friends in Vienna. Indigenous Tibetans hawkers display and sell excellent statues of Buddha, handmade silver jewellery, small knives and other curios on the footpaths. One can bargain with them and even without bargaining the prices are very reasonable. I buy a nice statue of Buddha that I shall put in my drawing room in Vienna.

The streets are crowded. Ali has many soldiers and immigrants from the Muslim part of China. The name of the city is changed from Shiquane to Ali, no wonder. The govern-

In Memory of the Passed Ones
(Photo by Dr. Hemant Mehta)

ment encourages and rewards their migration with sums of money in return for settling there. Most of the settlers are from southwest China bordering Pakistan. These settlers and the Chinese army defence force assigned to duty here eat meat. The local Buddhists are vegetarians and are strictly against butcher shops in the open market. These shops display lumps of slaughtered animals. Devout Buddhists are not only reluctant to kill an animal but are in great agony even to see the slaughtered displayed in piles of limbs. They close their eyes and murmur prayers when they pass by. While the Chinese wait, devour the lumps with their eyes and their mouths water. The faith conflict is pre-programmed. This is in the interest of the ruling government. The city has many brothels and discotheques. Wherever there are army barracks, these institutions come into life. These give rise to a moral dispute with the local conservative Buddhists. Business blooms in the city.

On my way back to the hotel, a small Chinese woman approaches me. She is a little creature in a chic dress. She talks to me in Chinese. I cannot understand a word of it. She follows me to the hotel. All the way I try to ignore her and make gestures that I do not understand her at all and she should go away. I arrive at the hotel followed by her. Vinodbhai makes fun of me. With a cynical smile on his face he asks, *where did you pick up this Devi (meaning devil)?* What I understand from her gestures is that that she has a restaurant in the city and she wants us to eat at her restaurant.

I understand she is looking for business. I direct the girl to Harishbhai, our leader. I am glad I get rid of her. She meets Harishbhai who discreetly sends her home. I notice one thing. Harishbhai who is usually very jolly and full of laughter, frowns at me and does not talk to me for a few hours. He displays his fury in a brief silence. Late in the evening Vinodbhai, Harishbhai and myself peep into a discotheque. In one remote dark corner, to my surprise, I see her once again, entertaining herself with some man. We hastily depart from the discotheque. I am anyway reluctant to go to a place where vitality overflows. I am writing this to warn all those who visit Tibet. I wish to warn them of the undercurrents that flow for a pilgrim even in remote places like Ali. To be ever conscious and to protect oneself is the right attitude. It is better to be old fashioned and right than to be dangerously extrovert and modern.

For us the day has come to an end. The long car journey has made us very tired. We have a massage at a hairdresser saloon and retire to the hotel. This is our second night in Ali. Ali leaves an impression of a city in conflict despite its lovely geographical position in the western mountains of Tibet. It is a strategic point of occupation since China sent troops in October 1950. Due to new immigration policies that have followed, Buddhists are losing their philosophical core to petty business ventures. For me, Ali in its present stage of development is disillusioning and a dreadful wound in the holy heart of torn Tibet.

On the 2 May, we bid farewell to Ali with a smile. We drive in a southeast direction to Gartok. Gartok was once a frequently visited town on the commercial route towards Trethapuri (Indians confidently call it Tirthapuri). Indians entering Tibet from the Indian side inevitably made a halt at Gartok. This is not true anymore. Since the Chinese occupation of Tibet this route is deserted and hence Gartok has lost its flair and importance. Apparently, Adi Shankracharya made a long journey to this part of the world to defend Hinduism against the then popular Buddhism. History is a witness that Buddhism is the greatest philosophical impetus that spread in the time. Unlike Islam and Christianity, it conquered the Eastern World without a sword. It would have really conquered the whole world, had the present modes of transportation and communication been available. A dozen high-

ranking Christians, Hindus and other missionaries came to
Tibet to convert the population to their faith. Their closer
association with Buddhism made them turn into Buddhists.

The Buddhist practice of meditation apparently conveys
and offers instant results. The main target of Buddhist meditation is to open the various *Chakras* (centres) of the being.
Once these Chakras start opening, not many ardent seekers
of reality can withstand the magnificent offer. Only
Shankaracharya was successful in convincing a Hindu king
not to convert to Buddhism in the interest of Hinduism. With
his influence, Shankracharya successfully confronted and
halted the conversion of the King's subjects in large num-
bers. A compromise with Buddhism was inevitable. In the
end Hinduism accepted Buddhism as a part of the great
Sanatan Dharma and claimed Buddha as an incarnation of
God. This was part of Hindu magnanimity. The religion that
came to challenge Hinduism was accepted as a part of
Hinduism. This way the dispute between Buddhism and
Hinduism was sorted out.

The name Shankaracharya stands tall in Hinduism. Since
then Trethapuri has became a place of great importance.
Shankaracharya's memories are still present at Trethapuri.
We arrive there in the early hours of the evening. Our camp,
including our kitchen and dining tent, four small sleeping
tents and the remote WC tent are tucked in the midst of hills
besides a glacial stream. This stream is none other than the
River Sutlej. At this stage the Sutlej is just a small stream. My
tent is tucked just a metre away from the bank of the river.
It is indeed a lovely place to rest. It soothes the mind to hear
the flowing water. For me it emanates divine music. In every
ripple and eddy of this lovely stream we feel the presence of
the great Creator.

Vinodbhai and myself go for an evening walk. We have a
wash at the hot sulphur and mineral spring. This is probably

the same pond where the great Shankracharya took his bath.
There are several hills on both sides of the banks of the
Sutlej. Once a year, on the opposite hill, gather all the holy
people of the neighbourhood to celebrate a feast. It is
indeed a lovely location for a spiritual vaudeville. I wish I
were able to participate in such a fiesta within the view of
the holy Thuling monastery. I am sure no spectacle can be
more sublime, serene and subtle. The Thuling monastery is
a place of historical significance for Tantric Buddhism and is
impressive with its powerful atmosphere. This is simply by
the virtue of its historical and tantric past practices that are
subdued at present. Now it appears deserted.

In the evening, in the main altar of the monastery I
arrange a puja for my late father to be performed by the
head of the monastery in the true Tibetan tradition. He
agrees to perform the puja and awaits no rewards. After he
finished his puja, listening to my inner voice Vinodbhai and
myself perform a Hindu puja. We sing an aarti. On comple-
tion I give the monk a *Dakshina* (gift in money). One
member of our group refutes the idea of performing a Hindu
ritual at a Buddhist shrine. He means that there is no rhyme
or reason to sing an aarti at a Buddhist shrine. Maybe he is
right. There is no real reason, not that I know of. But there
is definitely a rhyme in what we sing. This I assure you. We
sing and perform the aarti that is nowadays sung all over the
world, *Om Jai Jagdish Haré, Swami Jai Jagdish Haré* written
by the great Hindi poet Pundit Nathuram Shanker Sharma.[1]
This aarti is predominately a display of devotion in rhymes.
As a poem it is an excellent example of music in words. It
is normally sung in raag *Desh* that is exceedingly melodious
and arouses a feeling of extreme devotion.

My father was a very rational person. He did not believe

---

[1] Some Pundits attribute this aarti to Sadhu Shraddhanand, not identical
with Swami Shraddhanand of Arya Samaj.

in dogmatic worship of a deity. Still he believed in *Shraadh* (the Hindu ritual of remembering those who have passed away). I think this is the most befitting place to remember him, to perform his *Shraadh,* though these are not the days for performing Shraadh (*All Saints Day* for the Christians) according to the calendar. I feel my father's constant presence during the worship done in his memory. I carry his photo, along with my mother's, throughout the journey. They are present in this pilgrimage. Both of them are with me. My father was profoundly fond of travelling. Had he been alive he would have surely loved to be travelling with us, or even reading this account of my pilgrimage. I sense his acknowledgement of the ritual at the Thuling monastery. The atmosphere is spiritual. Many great Buddhist saints lived or came to this monastery and meditated. The presence of Buddha is constant here. The story of Bhramasambhava killing a demon with his tantric power and turning it to stone is dominating in the monastery. There are two uncut stones lying near the entrance. One large orange colour stone has the contour of an angel in action, killing a demon with a trident. The other stone, lying flat on the floor, appears to be the slain ogre. It is a light coloured stone with red splashes as if the demon is bleeding.

It is 3 May. It is a day of splendour. For the first time we see Kailash. We see it from far. I am utterly speechless, captured by its beauty. Looking at Kailash, the very moment I realise that I love Kailash more than I ever imagined. The encounter with Kailash is the most blissful event of my life. Kailash is my love at first sight. Tears of joy wet my eyes. It stirs my soul. Later in the night, while the world is asleep, this love of my soul spills on to paper in the form of a few lines that come to me out of nowhere. I note them down in my diary. Now when I type this on my keyboard, with minor alterations and an altered poetic enjambment, I realise it is a complete sonnet.

Chiu Gompa Monastery and Kailash
(Photo by the author)

KAILASH

Suddenly, through opulent light, Kailash is seen,
A million emotions capture my mind,
Bare Shiva wearing a snow-white pelerine,
In His serene beauty He turns my voice blind.

Though my speech is captive, my voice no tone,
I want to sing His song; Him I want to adore,
I want my song to reach from shore to shore,
Without His song, bliss of Love won't be won.

As a devotee I want to sing of His splendid hush,
Of His power in my spirit, deep in deep,
Of His abode from where four holy rivers[2] rush,
Giving glorious life to us, Him no sleep.

With my mortal speech still, how can I phrase
The heavenly grandeur of His glorious face?

Kailash is a mystic mountain indeed, in shape and surroundings. It *appears* (only appears) like a huge meteor that has settled there since time immemorial. This feeling I cannot conceal and I say it aloud to my group. My group expresses deep revulsion to such a thought. After a long silence one of them says,

> *There is a big danger in such a bizarre thinking as yours and it can cause a very wrong current of information that flows from mouth to mouth.*

To that I answer,

> *If there is a universal principal that this mountain is not to be climbed by anyone and no mountaineer has*

---

[2] The Karnali, the Brahmaputra, the Indus and the Sutlej.

*officially climbed its peak, then there must be some-
thing mysterious, something holy and something extraterritorial about it. It requires a new thinking to resolve
and search for the secret of this mystery. One who
reflects may tell aloud such new ideas and in this way
excite the interest of the researchers. There can be no
damage.*

He at once furiously opposes such thinking because it is
so not scientific. This reason is not explicit to me. Other
members of the group remain quiet. The distinctive mark of
a cultivated intellect is the willingness to examine, without
bias, a different opinion with flexibility of mind, poise of
feeling and calmness of judgement. At some point, I am
bound to ask them for forgiveness for my liberal thinking. I
do it. I do not care to continue this controversy. This is
contrary to my uncompromising nature. My life is a long
lesson in humility. It is hard but fruitful to learn that the real
fruits of humility are love and peace. I am on a pilgrimage.
There is no true pilgrimage without love and peace. My
journey to Tibet would prove futile if I participated in the
slightest conflict. The true felicity of life is to be free from
perturbations and aggression. To have harmony and hold
onto my pilgrim's approach, I apologise to each one in the
group. As I am the youngest in the group, this is considered
a gesture of good social upbringing.

Still, I strongly feel that my premise is right. Kailash really
appears like a meteor. One may charge me for want of sense
and still I would loudly say that the least approach to a false
pretence is not amongst my sins. Our group does not keep
the idea open for discussion since it is *l'idée nouvelle*.
Though I live in a fantasy world, my thinking is now based
on reasons that I think are relevant factors.

Most of the mountains I have seen are part of the range
of mountains. The Austrian Alps are a range and so are also
the Himalayan ranges. This cannot be said of Kailash though

there is a small Kailash range of hills around. The photographs of Kailash also prove the veracity of this fact. Kailash
as a mountain is unique. It stands solitary, majestic like a
pyramid. It gives an impression of an extraterritorial object.
It has a rounded peak. Its colour is a lustrous black - grey,
only a flush of grey on the muzzle. One gets a constant
feeling that Kailash has some magnetic currents around it as
if it contains iron ore. Or is it really a meteor that has
collected magnetic power in its journey towards Earth?

All these make Kailash different from others. Still, one
may ask, is it sufficient to make Kailash so holy? It has
enjoyed its sacred reputation since very early times of history. There must be some different reason for this attribute
given to it. May be with time we have forgotten it.

The key to the mystery may be as simple as ever. Our
world has always worshipped extraterritorial objects. There
is no doubt about it. Many of the world's holy icons
devotedly worshipped by Christians, Muslims and Hindus
are apparently extraterritorial meteors. The loving and com-
passionate black Madonna of Montserrat in Spain, the shining and powerful Holy Ka'bah of Mecca, the living and
breathing Sri Nathji (Sir Lord) of Nathdwara with His eyes
keeping us under divine surveillance, are all forms of black
stone, apparently from meteors. Kailash is an object of
worship as far as our memory takes us back. Shiva is
traditionally and symbolically worshipped in the temples as
Shiva Linga, again a black stone. There are sure reasons for
such symbols attributed to Shiva whose abode is Kailash.
The question remains - is Kailash extraterritorial? I wish
some scientist would work to prove this theory. I am definitely going to dig deep into the subject once I am at home.
A wise sage once said,

> *That which can be made explicit to everyone is not
> worth any care. The wisest of the ancients considered,
> what is not so explicit as the fittest for instructions,
> because it rouses the faculties to act.*

This should be enough reason for many to investigate this mystery. I believe that in the search of truth, it is evident that no one will master or miss it wholly. Each controversy will add a little to our awareness. When all the facts are assembled then it will ascend to certain grandeur. This grandeur will suffice to live for a long time until new facts are added to it.

There is another strange feature of Kailash. On the south face of Kailash one notices some deep horizontal cuts in the mountain stone. These cuts give the impression of a stair-case, a staircase that is rising to heaven. The Hindu scriptures have very often mentioned about a staircase to heaven. We are all aware of it in our minds. I wonder if it tallies with this staircase. We all know the legend of *Mahabharata*. *Yudhistir* (also called Dharam Raj) climbed the steps with his faithful dog and knocked at the gates of heaven. Apparently *Maryada Purshottam Rama Dasharati of Ayodhya* also climbed the staircase to heaven. Were these the steps of Kailash? If you visit a Shiva temple and observe the Shiva Linga, it is marked with three white lines, which are drawn horizontal on the black linga. Worshippers of Shiva also mark their foreheads with three horizontal lines as a sign of third eye leading to a mysterious horizon. I wonder if this has something to do with the horizontal cuts on Kailash.

When, in history, is the beginning of this reverence for Kailash? The question also remains, why is Kailash equally holy for Buddhists and Hindus. Why are there restrictions to climb it? Why are the Gods and great saints the exceptions? All accept this belief that Kailash should not be climbed. The governments of India, Tibet and China respect this religious view. Even today no permission is granted to climb the peak of Kailash. Why can one go around Kailash in parikrama or cora as the Tibetans do and not climb it? When did the association of Kailash with divinity start? These are the questions that arise for which I have no answers. Hence I lay them safely at the feet of Lord Shiva who sits here in

An Artist's Conception of Lord Shiva
(Artist unknown)

Mansarovar - west shore
(Photo by the author)

perpetual meditation. He does not answer me. I cannot get
over the feeling that Kailash is mystic and divine in it
appearance.

We photograph Kailash a thousand times from Chiu
Gompa, the monastery. This monastery is situated in a very
remote area with only a few monks living there. It has a
tantric appeal. The constellation of Kailash, Mount Gurla
Mandhata (7728 metres), named after a rishi who did tapasya
here, and holy Mansarovar is fascinating. This triangle brings
a feeling of some mystic magnetic field, which latently flows,
under the ground. To learn the usage of this magnetic field
one has to sit at a particular angle and invoke some centres
of the body by rubbing them. In this way one summons and
invokes the Gods residing in ones own body with the help
of a magnetic muscle that is in the atmosphere. This leads to
an unusual aid in the practice of meditation. This is the
secret knowledge that is not at the disposal of everyone. It
requires years of assimilation of yogic powers to enable the
practice of this yoga. The Chiu Gompa monastery probably
has or had this knowledge.

The monastery stands high on a hill between two lakes.
Mansarovar (Brahma's Lake) and Rakshas Tal (Ravana's
Lake). The atmosphere is very mystical here. Its location
itself is of great interest for students of esoteric studies. In the
narrow passage between these two lakes is a gold mine. The
Chinese discovered it and it is now a regular source of gold.
It is no secret that Tibet is exceptionally rich in minerals,
metals and semi-precious stones. The Chinese are exploiting
this natural richness of Tibet. The world has also suddenly
discovered Tibet. Tibet is a gold mine as a tourist attraction.
They are now concentrating on preserving Tibetan culture to
earn money from tourism. Enough monasteries have been
destroyed during the Cultural Revolution. According to the
Hollywood mega film *Seven Years in Tibet*, starring Brad Pitt,
six thousand monasteries were uprooted. Nearly one million
Tibetans lost their lives during the revolution. A lot of

children died too. Amongst these children, how many
infants with the future realization of Nagarjun, Gandhi,
Einstein, Beethoven and Krishnaprem have departed, while
the world watched, no one can verify today. Forever, mankind is poorer for this loss. Who can assess the extent of
knowledge that was lost in the six thousand monasteries?

It is a wonder that the Chiu Gompa is one monastery that
has survived the upheaval and is now maintained. From this
monastery you can see Kailash on one side and the banks of
the Mansarovar and Rakshas Tal on the other side. Rakshas
Tal is a lake that Hindu mythology considers as the seat of
demons (antithesis). It is a little lower than Mansarovar and
darker in colour. No life exists in the Rakshas Tal while
Mansarovar has an exceptionally large range of aquatic life.
Strange, but true, that in the vicinity of this monastery,
Kailash as witness, between the Mansarovar and Rakshas
Tal, more on the side of Mansarovar, Morari Bapu had his
Ram katha. This incident has such a symbolic significance.
Ramcharitmanas (literally translated - the study of the
character of Rama) is a saga of Rama, Divine Incarnation of
Vishnu on one side and the demonic destructive and still
enlightened power Ravana on the other side. Rama is God
personified and Ravana is the fallen angel as his character
is wicked even though he has attained enlightenment
and boon of immortality from *Brahma* on the shores of
Rakshas Tal.

Today is 4 May. We are at Darchen. We begin the
parikrama (circling) of Kailash in the early hours. After a
short joint prayer with Jagdishbhai as our pilot, we commence
the march. Vinodbhai and myself begin the parikrama with
a worshipful repose and prayer wheels in our hands turning
them in a clockwise motion, as the Buddhist pilgrims do. I
constantly chant the mahamantra of the Hindus, *Om Namah
Shivaya* (concentrating on you, O Lord of creation, I bow
down to you). We have a Gurkha who carries our cameras
and extras. This leaves us to concentrate on meditation. The

Kailash - A Staircase to Heaven
(Photo by the author)

Vinod and the Author resting while circling the Kailash
(Photo by Dr. Hemant Mehta)

sky is a sapphire stretch of vastness and the mighty holy Kailash is in full glory. We look at the west face of Kailash so close to us. We cannot have enough of this view.

Kailash is the source of four mighty rivers - Karnali, Brahmaputra, Indus and Sutlej. Karnali springs from the north face of Kailash. A stream of Karnali eventually joins many other streams and is the source of the holy Ganges at Gaumukh that is 13 miles southwest from Gangotri. Hence mythology accounts that Ganges spurts from the matted hair on the head of Shiva. The Karnali stream of water that flows from Kailash into Ganges makes the Ganges holy.

I continually look and wonder about Kailash during the three-hour walk from Darchen to Chiku (Choku) Gompa monastery. We camp there. The more I see the more I begin to wonder. I ask myself again and again if this is an extraterritorial meteor. In the evening it turns really windy and cold. The cold hits us hard as soon as the sun starts setting. I am stunned by the vision of a golden sunset, the sun spraying a *rangoli* of colours from the west on Kailash in front of us. The sky is a painter's full canvas of different shades of pink, purple, yellow and gold. It looks so artificial, as if God has created computer graphics. Everyone else is tired and shows signs of emotional fatigue, as the day stretches out with overwhelming beautiful images. I take a photo of Kailash. I am full of enthusiasm even though my mind remains saturated with impressions. I have an innovative thought. I prepare my camera with the intention of making pictures of Kailash in the night. Dipl. Ing. Prof. Walter Tschiedel, an Austrian whose friends I met in Lhasa, has taken an excellent photo of Kailash framed with twinkling stars. His friends described it in German as *wunderschön, Kitsch und unglaublich* (wonderful, rugged and unbelievable). I have not seen the photo. From its description I wish to take such a photo. I load my Nikon with ASA 800 film.

I go early to bed with the intention of getting up in the night without anyone noticing and sneaking out to make the

A Glimpse of Kailash
(Photo by Dr. Hemant Mehta)

Kailash at Night
(Photo by Dipl. Ing. Prof. Walter Tschiedel of Austria)

most unusual photos of the trip. Before going to sleep I peep
outside from my sleeping bag that has been warmed with a
hot water bottle. Suddenly the sky has changed. The clear
sky of the day has vanished. There are no close stars but a
silent milky sky that speaks of snow. It appears as if it is
going to snow during the next few hours. I wonder if I have
to surrender my secret mission.

I feel my head with my palm. I still have a slight tempera-
ture, a headache and my body is restless. I am unable to
sleep. The whole night I am in a state of delirium. I close my
eyes to fall asleep. My mind engages itself with the idea of
taking the photos, but my body is not supportive at all. I
think I am in a different psychological world. As I cannot
sleep, I engage in meditation, my breathing becomes harder.
The tent has very little oxygen, as the altitude is high. I
hopelessly try to pull my spirit out of my body. I forget for
a short moment, in the upward pull straining my mind, that
I am doing something. Suddenly I find that I am in a
hospital. It is a very confusing and a perturbing situation. I
can see my body lying on an operation table, paralyzed - as
if dead - and I am perfectly conscious. It is not as if I am
dreaming. When one dreams things are in a misty ambience,
above reasons. One slithers in the flow of events regardless
of one's desire. Here I am conscious. I am in complete
possession of my spirit. I am able to use my will. I am fully
aware that I am being operated for the problem of nocturia.
Somebody gives me a spinal injection. I feel the prick and
the piercing pain. The injection gives me instant numbness
that steadily but inexorably creeps up in my whole body. I
am panting for breath. I feel that something has gone terribly
wrong with me. I hear somebody saying that *the patient is
withdrawing*. The doctor who is operating on me is Hemant
Mehta. Dr. Mrinalini Mehta is assisting him. She runs helter-
skelter. I see a Tibetan nurse feeling my pulse. Vinodbhai in
a white coat is administrating oxygen. I realize what this
means. I realize my time is ending. I meditate on my third
eye as I do every morning and chant

ॐ तत् सवितुर्वरं रूपं ज्योति: परस्य धीमहि ।
यन्न: सत्येन दीपयेत् ।।

श्री अरविंद

Om tat saviturvaram rupam jyoti parasy dhimahi
Yannah satyana dipyet.

Sri Aurobindo

Let us meditate on the most auspicious,
form of The Creator,
on the light of the Supreme which shall,
illumine us with the Truth.

Translation—Sri Aurobindo,
the sage/poet himself

There is no sign of anxiety in my being. I am cheerful. Angst is absent and so is Amita, my wife. I know Amita is far away in Vienna. Still, I want to see her once before I leave. I want to bid her farewell. I know that afterwards I may never again meet her in this person. I cannot simply leave without meeting her. She is a very good partner and I have progressed much in her partnership. I say this to Hemantbhai. He shakes his head. Dr.Mrinalini dressed in a white coat and stethoscope smiles and consoles me. *Be not frightened. We will pull you out of this.* I want to speak further. A hiccup intervenes. I feel that a hiccup at this stage surely signifies death. Without hesitation I smile and say, *my friends, you have been very kind. You have tried exceptionally hard to help me. You have done all you can. What can one do when He personally steps in to call it a day for me? I thank you for your compassion and solicitude. Let me bid farewell to you.* I feel the numbness is getting closer to my chest; so much so that I think it is my last breath. I have always wished to go intact, with full presence of my mind. Curiously at this time I want to test my mind if it is clear and active as ever. I remember the context of a sloka from the Bhagwad Gita. Sri Krishna assures,

अन्तकाले च मामेव स्मरन्मुक्त्वा कलेवरम् ।
य: प्रयाति स मद्भंव याति नास्यत्र संशय ।।

भगवत् गीता ८:५

Antakale ch mamev smaranmuktvakalevarm,
Yah prayati se medbhavam yati nastytre samshyah.

One who remembers Me in his last breath at
the point of leaving,
The body, rest assured shall merge back total in
My being......

BHAGWAT GITA, 8:5

Then I recite silently my favorite lines from Sri Aurobindo's
Savitri:

I smite the Titan who bestrides the world,
And slay the ogre in his blood-stained den,
I am Durga, Goddess of the proud and strong,
And Lakshmi, the queen of the fair and fortunate.

SRI AUROBINDO – *Savitri Book,* 7:4

On reciting these powerful lines, a profound peace
descends on my entire being. A light and a power penetrate
through my slumberous body. I slowly gain power as if
Durga has strengthened my entire being and made me
strong. Has poetry or mantra so much force? A marvel profoundly proceeds. I, who happened to be at the porch of a
latent land from where no traveler ever returns, have come
back.

I open my eyes, I see Vinodbhai in the tent. He is sound
asleep. My first feeling is one of bounding happiness. No
one can imagine how joyful I am to see him. At this stage I
decide to remain silent about this dream. I consider the
whole incident as an esoteric experience. I realize there is

nothing that belongs to us permanently. If my health is now restored, it is restored only to express the well of my sentient being. My urge to strive for happiness is only temporary. For temporary remains the material happiness. Only soul or Atma is Always.

This is an experience that I want to keep only for myself. I note it down in my diary, thinking that at a later stage I may narrate it only to my family and friends. The strange thing about this dream is that I had a very similar dream in Vienna years before, though with a different set of players. What it signifies, I have not the faintest idea. It is a riddle for a student of Jungian psychology to interpret. I decisively leave this dream-travel in limbo and attend to the wonderful nature around me. When I peep out of the tent it is dawn. The sky is classic glittery grey as if it is a projection of a Hollywood mega film. It has snowed. I am not able to take the photos of Kailash at night; this I regret. I wonder why this had to happen. Why should the Lord intervene in this manner, I am unable to say. I accept His Will without any reservations. There is a divinity that controls our actions and shapes our ends. We have just to stand, watch and let it work without any qualms. Our duty is to continue to remain happy.

The next day, 5 May, we walk to Diraphuk Gompa Monastery. The walk is long. At one point we have to cross a frozen river. Our Gurkha, who is very experienced, leads us. I am constantly faced with the scenario that if I step on the thin layer of breaking ice, I will be knee-deep in frozen water. The winds are so cold that if any such accident happens it would deteriorate my health considerably and I won't be able to enjoy the rest of the pilgrimage. I am very careful. Nothing like such fantasy happens. In the dusk of the Himalayan world, we camp at the foot of the Diraphuk monastery. We get up to see that it has snowed heavily. Dolma La (Drollma La) pass above us is dangerous to traverse. The chances of continuing parikrama are getting slimmer. It is slippery and the likelihood of an accident

cannot be ruled out. We really consider getting a herd of
yaks to help us clear the snow to let us complete the
parikrama. We have come so far and we want to continue.
We want to see the North face of Kailash, which gives us
excellent opportunities to take beautiful photos of the holy
mountain, as we are closest. We stay one more night in the
camp.

In the evening we meet the Lama of the Diraphuk Gompa
Monastery. He is a burly young man, round and well fed.
We have a joint meditation with him. His forehead is full of
light and his chanting of the rhythmic mystic words of
Buddhism in his metallic voice carries me far in the meditation.
Before I close my eyes for meditation I notice that Mrinalben,
Jagdishbhai and Vinodbhai are in deep meditation. Kunjbhai
and Hemantbhai are busy photographing. Kunjbhai, as I
have noticed till now, is a very keen photographer and he
strives to be perfect. Hemantbhai is a person with few
words. He speaks only when it is necessary. He is a
photographer of distinction and is a fellow of the Royal
Society of Photographers. The occasion offers a perfect
opportunity to register images. At one point Hemantbhai
leaves his camera and is fully submerged in the meditative
atmosphere. I think he is meditating with open eyes. His
power of concentration is immense and has the strength of
a very developed soul. This feeling I get only when I look
closely at him.

The ambience of the Lama is very pleasant. His Lamasery
is exactly facing Kailash. The native Tibetans who are doing
cora come to rest here. He gives them shelter, food and tea
around the clock. These pilgrims are usually on the cora for
many days. The posture and ritual of cora is very strenuous.
Standing erect, folding your hands stretching towards high
heaven as if praying for the grace from above; then bringing
the folded hands to the heart as if enclosing His blessings in
the heart, then lowering the folded hands to the limbs as if
transferring the divine strength to the body, they lie down

flat on the floor in total surrender to God. Step forward to the place where stretched hands touch the floor and then the rituals start again.

With each gesture they chant the mantra *Om Mani padme Hum*. This means *'Hail to the Jewel in the Lotus.'* This Jewel in the Lotus (body) is nothing but the soul, the divine spark within us. So they constantly invoke the God while the body is being prepared for *Its* manifestation. These rituals immensely help those who generally identify themselves only with the body. With these rigorous rituals, they seek a ceaseless awareness of the component parts of their thoughts, minds and bodies so that eventually they can wholly free themselves from the illusion of being only the body. They endeavour to identify themselves with the soul, *Jewel (mani—* मणि*)* inside the body. This practice of marching around Kailash is called cora. And this is done in all weather conditions, even stretching one's body flat in the snow. We met, saw and talked to many pilgrims doing cora with such vigorous postures. Absolute devotion and firm conviction in Kailash can only be the source of such arduous rituals.

Some of these elderly pilgrims need a rest after every hour or two. Even when they rest, they turn their prayer wheels in clockwise motion with prayers. They pray to be out of the constant cycle of birth and death. The material world is, for them evanescent. सर्वं शून्यं । सर्वं क्षणिकम् ।। (All amounts to zero. All is momentary) as Buddha used to say, in his princely Sanskrit to confirm his क्षणिकवाद (the theory that this material world is ephemeral). To enter a state of everlasting divine joy, one has to be liberated from this world and enter Nirvana. These pilgrims are on a march to discover Nirvana, a consciousness that will banish grief and suffering forever. They seek the portal to immortality.

Such are the pilgrims who come to the monastery for a pause. It may take them from fifteen days to a month to finish the cora around Kailash. A large number of pilgrims do it every year. The Lama gives them shelter, food and protection. When we see all this in front of our eyes, we cannot but help fold our own hands to these pilgrims and the Lama in absolute adoration.

From the terrace of his monastery one literally touches Kailash through the floating clouds. The Lama has the sheer joy of living face to face with so gallant a friend, Shiva, though remote from civilisation. This situation he really hugs to his heart. He tells me that with the gestures of his hands and a complacent smile on his face. He even gives me a private audience in his study room where we meditate together for a while and he blesses me with a smile and an affirmative nod of his head. This gesture is beyond my comprehension. He gives me *prasad* (meditated piece of toffee) to carry back home. He gives a Katha (silk scarf) to each one of us. While meditating with him alone, I pray for the light inside me and not for the betterment of the weather. I am determined to accept God's will as far as the circling of Kailash is concerned. Still, our joint patience is pointed to one aspiration - that is for a positive weather improvement.

On the 6th it is equally grey, cold and Kailash is totally lost in the gloomy mist of the clouded sky. We see only fragments of the mountain in front of us. We decide to return to our base camp. Our decision is based on logic. Even if we take a risk and go around Kailash, we are unable to see the grandeur of the holy mountain. So why take the risk just for the sake of an irrational religious belief to go around it? The religion probably connected the circling with heavenly reward for those men who needed to be awakened from inertia and see God's creation. The religious awards were to motivate them to see the grandeur of nature. We want to see Kailash and we have travelled a long way to do the circling of Kailash. Still, for us there is no alternative but to retreat. We are sad that we cannot finish our circling of Kailash. We console ourselves with the argument that we have walked twice the same half of the full circle. These two halves are

to be considered as one full encirclement by the benevolent
Lord.

On 7 May, we march back to the Chiu Gompa monastery
camping place where our jeeps pick us up. It is windy, ice
cold and depressing. The walk back is the longest walk of
my life as my feet are sore, cold and full of fatigue. Mrinalini
is the last one to join us at the place where we are waiting
for our jeeps. The ferocious winds blow through our bones.
We protect ourselves in a shield of rocks lying on the
ground. Each of us is wearing at least four to six layers and
still it is cold. We retreat to Darchen guesthouse. It is
depressing because we had to break up our march around
the holy mountain. Who can control the weather? I comfort
myself by remembering a sloka of the Bhagwad Gita.

तस्मादपरिहार्येऽर्थे न त्वं शोचितुमर्हसि

भगवत् गीता, २:२७

Tasmadapariharyerthe na tvam shochitumharsi

Over that which is inevitable Thou shall not grieve.

(BHAGWAT GITA, 2:27)

Though we have come so far, we should accept life as it
comes our way without grievances. I divert my attention to
other things. I collect some black stones at the foot of
Kailash. These shall be put into my prayer and meditation
enclosure in Vienna. I shall have a small memento of Kailash
at home.

Today is 8 May. We are back at Darchen guesthouse. I
meet Brahmchari Sadhu Rajendra. He is youthful and has
come from India without any support, visa or even proper
shoes and clothing. A Lama has given him some trousers. On
his left hand he has only one glove that somebody gave him.
He has thin-soled summer canvas shoes and is inadequately
clothed for the cold ambience of the Lord. Still his face
reflects that genuine *joie de vivre*-He is a happy person and

that is why joy spouts out from his soul like natural spring
water. His heart is all love and warmth for Kailash. He lives
with his firm fervour and the power derived from it that
Shiva lives on top of Kailash and he is meeting Him everyday. He has no money and no way to affirm what or where
he shall eat his next meal. His devotion to Shiva is unflinch-
ing. He meditates long hours. His forehead has a dent at the
same place where Indian ladies do their chandla (tika). I feel
his third eye will open soon. I like him. I feel he is very
sincere.

I show my reverence for his saintly character and gentle,
gracious manners. There is magnetism in his personality, and
an impalpable aura of a lofty ideal about him, which leaves
a deep impression on me. Calm and reserved, he is the
centre of respectful attention. To talk to him is to be inspired.
His voice is mellow and his Hindi honey. His presence
radiates something that is at once enlivening and exalting.
His influence springs from his unshakable peace that spouts
from the secret of his utter self-effacement. He is youthful.
Still, at such a young age, maturity is portrayed in his person.
He looks so genuine. His magnitude is like the mild breath
of a Kailash cold-water spring, invisible but alluring.
Jagdishbhai, Mrinalben and myself show reverence to him
even though he is very young. I feel the rest of my group
does not give him much significance. This, I think, makes
our group a little narrow in our opening to other influences
except that of the magical Himalayan world. Sadhu Rajendra
intends to go around Kailash one hundred and eight times.
This, he thinks, will make him stalwart spiritually. On the
day we, who are equipped with the best of the western
warm attire, retreated from our parikrama, he passed the
Golma La Pass with his canvas shoes and completed his
circling of Kailash.

He is a man worthy of wonder. Not because he is going
around Kailash one hundred and eight times in all weather
conditions but because of his stupendous faith in Shiva.

Brahmchari Sadhu Rajendra and the Author
(Photo by Jigme)

There is a look of ecstasy in his eyes as he tells me that while circling Kailash everyday, he meets an Indian lady (Yogini) who has lived in the caves of Kailash for more than a hundred years to meditate strenuously. A gush of cold winds blow into my face and I shiver. My eyes are wet with tears. I wonder how many more mysteries Shiva holds in His chest? I have a photo taken with Sadhu Rajendra.

On 9 May, we are ready to drive to the east shore of Mansarovar and camp there. If you look at the map of Mansarovar, we are exactly facing Chiu Gompa monastery where we had been initially. The drive is not long. The sun shines most benignly, emanating light but not heat. I remove my jacket and sweater to let sunlight flood on myself. The air is crisp. Once the sun sets it is ice cold, with the Mansarovar winds blowing deep inside our bones. Mansarovar is the highest freshwater lake in the world. We are at 4550 metres above sea level. Having this dream come true so utterly has given me enormous gratification. We are all in the sweep of the one and only *Love for the All Beautiful* enveloping us totally. I have become a motionless mound, my face tucked among layers of blue white colours above the horizon where a pot of pure gold pours with immense craft. Behind me are rocks and stones with tufts of spear grass. In front of me glacier–flanked peaks of Kailash (known as Kangrinboque Feng to the Tibetans) rise abruptly, the holiest and among the highest peaks in the world. Kailash - a complete embodiment of universal power, the cosmic centre of the universe.

Kailash is a creative force of unimaginable dimensions. This is precisely why it is the abode of Shiva, the creative force. *He* sits here for millions of human years, waking up only to create a new universal order and probably act to effect the change of equinoxes. Why does *He* do it? What is the power behind this Universal Order? This is an eternal question of metaphysics. All my fantasy fails to answer me. While I am searching for an answer, four powerful lines of the Italian poet Dante Alighieri from *Divina Commedia - Paradiso* flash before me.

A l'alta fantasia qui mancó possa,
Ma già volgeva il mio disio e 'l velle,
Si come rota ch'igualmente è mossa,
L'amor che move il sole e l'altre stelle.

The vigor failed the towering fantasy,
Yet, like a wheel whose speed no tremble mars,
Desire rushed on, its spur unceasingly,
The Love that moves the sun and the other stars.

(Divine Comedy - Paradise)
(Translation: Amal Kiran)

It is God's *l'amor* (in the last line of Dante), the *love* of Shiva for us that is the strength that moves the sun, the moon and the stars. He creates the Universal Order. The ancient Indian Rishis visualised this form in the dancing Shiva or Natraj. The name Natraj means the *King Actor*. He is the king actor in the perfect play of our universe. The statue of Natraj, so much worshipped by artists, especially dancers, symbolises the Big Bang Theory of the Universe. Becoming aware of this meaningful vision of the ancient Rishis, I feel assured that Shiva is Kailash and Kailash is Shiva. In Kailash is embodied the power of Shiva. I wonder how would He look when He is awake and dancing. I ask our *Varishta Neta* (senior guide). He tells me - *Don't think of Shiva's dance. It is destruction colossal first.*

At present it is the feeling of constant All Beautiful that is dominant here. The most beautiful thing we can experience here is the mysterious. He who is an alien to this emotion, who has not learnt to pause, to wonder and to stand, wrapped in marvel at this mysterious heavenly ambience is totally blind. The insight into the mystery of life, though at times coupled with fear, gives rise to faith. To know that *That* which is impenetrable to us, really exists. At times it is perceived by the sixth sense, which is often beyond reason. Often it manifests itself as the most radiant divine splendour

and our limited faculties strive to comprehend. It manifests
in their most ancient form mainly as described in the scriptures of all religions. This knowledge is the centre of religion. This is how Hinduism and Buddhism associate this
place with the divine. Before me, down on Earth, is the
heavenly Mansarovar (also known as Brahma's Lake), a
sacred reality where Shiva attained His Godly attributes. At
this point I still wonder if Shiva with his creative, preserva-
tive and destructive forces is an allegory for Kailash or a
historical fact with all His immense powers of destruction. It
is so perfect, pure and peaceful here. I am totally submerged
in the impact of Kailash.

There are innumerable spiritual personalities who have
visited this place. Amongst these are Bhagwan Sri
Swaminarayan, Baba Balaknath and many more. Jagdishbhai
chants some Sanskrit mantras. Mrinalini and myself devotedly join the sort of extempore puja (ceremonial worship). I
try to meditate deep inside me just to hear my own loud
breathing. The thumb like flame that resides inside my chest,
by the side of the heart, is unreachable despite my devoted
efforts. I hope that the powerful magnetic field of the pilgrim
soil where I stand works as a turbo power to my ardent
efforts to reach inside me. I am determined to rise above
rationality and absorb the pilgrimage in full faith. I do not go
far in meditation except to quiet myself. I feel disappointed
for a moment. I have been trying to pray and meditate for
years, since my childhood and still I have not reached far. I
feel that I am too opaque to the inward ray of light. As my
endeavours fail me, I open my eyes. I realise that only
Jagdishbhai and Mrinalini are engrossed in deep meditation.
Mrinalini has tears in her eyes, gazing at Kailash, sprinkling
the holy and lucid waters of Mansarovar. I feel Jagdishbhai
is transported away in meditation. I think he is far, far with
Shiva who sits on the top of Kailash in perpetual meditation.
After an interval that appears long, Mrinalini and myself bow
down to Jagdishbhai in turns for his blessings. Jagdishbhai is
the most senior member of the group. He grants us blessings
with the grand Kailash as our divine witness.

Jagdishbhai Trivedi Blessing the Author
(Photo by Dr. Mrinalini Mehta)

Subsequently, all three of us gaze at the snow flaked Kailash. Hemantbhai is at the far end, not heeding our presence or rituals. Kunjbhai is busy framing his prize shots with his exclusive range of cameras. There are .neither white swans swimming in the lucid celestial water nor is the lake full of water lilies or lotus blooms. I do not see them at all. The *white swan* is a poetic and spiritual symbol of *purity* and the *lotus* (the seat of Saraswati - the goddess of knowledge, arts and speech) is the spiritual symbol of *perfection*. *Purity and perfection* are floating everywhere in the air. One cannot fail to feel it. Mansarovar, as the name suggests, was born out of the mind (manas) of the creator of the universe, Brhama. A mystic power is indeed dominating the atmosphere. Vinodbhai and Harishbhai are at the far western end, knee deep in Mansarovar. Since the beginning of this expedition Vinodbhai and Harishbhai have developed a bond of close friendship. Vinodbhai is filming Harishbhai and chanting the Gayatri Mantra attributed to the grand sage and poet Vishwamitra.

ॐ भूर्भुवः स्वः तत्सवितुर्वरेण्यम् ।
भर्गो देवस्य धीमही
धियो यो नः प्रचोदयात् ।।

Om Bhur Bhuva Suwaha,
Tat[3] Savitur[4] Varenyam,
Bhargo Devasya Dhimahee,
Dhiyo Yo Nah Pracho Dayat.

Let us meditate,
On the most excellent Light,
Of the Divine Truth,
That it may impel our minds,
Without reserve.

---

[3] Tat - The Absolute, Transcendent, containing all, limited by nothing.
[4]The epistemological meaning of Savitur is derived from the word "Su" meaning in Sanskrit to give birth.
Savitur- The Creator, here seen as The Mother Force.

Vinod Budhdeo and the Author Praying at Mansarovar
(Photo by Chandra)

I keenly observe everyone around in my ambience. That is because I wish to include a lot of details in the notes that I write in the late hours of the night before I go to sleep. After jotting down a few code words I turn back to my ardent efforts to meditate. I look at Kailash and give tributes and pronounce gratitude to my forefathers with the holiest of the holy waters. Had it not been for them I would not be. Without my existence how would I have ever experienced such a deep spiritual atmosphere today? Hindus and Buddhists firmly believe in life after death and immortality of the soul. Some of them believe that their forefathers live on the Kailash, snugly under His direct protection.

Vinodbhai has an amazing idea. He has prepared sheets of papers with the names of family members. We make paper boats of these letters. These boats are floated in the Mansarovar to be sent to Shiva. These are our love letters for our dear ones who dwell with Him. He also floats letters on behalf of all his friends in the world. I also imagine that my forefathers are also up on Kailash with Him. I send them a letter. I also let my letter float in the Mansarovar. In this letter I thank Lord Shiva for protecting my forefathers. Then I pull myself up closer to Him. I give Him the highest attributes given to a God. I look high at Him and call out:

त्वमेव माता च पिता त्वमेव
त्वमेव बंधुश्च सखा त्वमेव
त्वमेव विद्या द्रविणं त्वमेव
त्वमेव सर्वं मम् देव देव।

गुरु गीता

Tvamev Mata ch Pita tvamev,
Tvamev Bandhush ch Sakha tvamev,
Tvamev Vidya, Dravidam tvamev,
Tvamev Sarvam mum Dev, Dev.

(From the collection of prayers GURU GITA)

Author Paying Tributes to His Forefathers at Mansarovar
(Photo by Dr. Mrinalini Mehta)

You - my Father and Mother in one,
My comrade, friend and All in all,
My wisdom, light and dearest pearl,
My God of gods, To You I call.

He answers my call with a still more expanded silence. I feel like a traveller between the summit and the abyss buried in the remnants of the forgotten past. I wish some God would answer my call. I am given to understand that this stark and desolate wilderness is home to innumerable deities and holy men.

I meditate on Lord Sri Ramchandra who came to Kailash-Mansarovar. I think of virtuous Vibhishan, the war ally of Sri Rama who also attained some spiritual powers here, so says the legend. Adjacent to Mansarovar is Rakshas Tal, Ravana's Lake. As the name suggests, this is in the valley of Rakshas, or the divine antithesis. Inevitably, and against my grain, I also think of Ravana the divine antithesis, the Ravana of Golden Lanka who attained his immortality here at the Rakshas Tal by his extensive tapasya. Only Sri Rama, who was an incarnation of Lord Vishnu, could kill Ravana. After completing his mission on the earth Sri Rama apparently climbed the steps of Kailash leading Him to heaven. Facing Kailash, behind me is the mount Gurla Mandhata (7,728 metres). Further to the west and south, beyond the border, over the mountains on the Indian side, next to the side of the holy city of Badrinath, is the famous Valley of Flowers. Still further southwards, on the same longitude as Kailash, is the holy city of Allahabad or Prayag.

Jigme, our indigenous Tibetan guide, tells me that there is a legend that on every full moon night, Parvati, the consort of Lord Shiva, descends down to bathe in the Mansarovar. She looks radiantly beautiful. I think this may be an allegory making *la nuit, La Belle Dame de Seigneur Shiva* (the night, the beautiful consort of Lord Shiva). I hear that on the full moon the night emanates a silver and mauve glow that

Mount Gurla Mandhata with Mansarovar
(Photo by the author)

reflects from the snow above into the clear waters of Mansarovar. The description of the beauty of the night bathing and reflecting in Mansarovar and its glory is thrilling. For me it is too icy to come and watch in the night. It is also not a full moon night now. The lake has an historic exist-ence of millions of aeon years but it is so tranquil and turquoise at this moment that it is almost dumb in its ambience.

A lone sheep is drinking the clear divine water at the far end of lake as if it has not heeded us at all. Another herd of sheep leisurely heading down the valley passes by me. Then the slope is silent. I climb the hill upwards almost afloat in the bright light. I regret I am not carrying a camera. There are a few white clouds in the sky. The sky is azure, stretched infinitely towards the horizon.

Suddenly there occurs a movement of the May blizzard somewhere distant but still so near. It sounds to me like a sudden messenger from the all-seeing tops that traverse the soundless corridors of my mind. It looks like a nude arm of spiritual splendour suddenly rising and renting the gauze opaque of wilderness. The ether is full of motion. The magical air brings its rhythmic sense of latent things from the hidden peaks of the heights of the mighty Kailash to us. Music floats, transcending mortal speech as if from a golden height of All-Bliss. The sun is overpowering as if it is so near and still remains non-measuring. There is a joy of light, a joy of sight and a rapture of thrilling Himalayan Holy World.

All my words are futile to describe the celestial beauty descended on Earth. It is so unfortunate that our experiences cannot be transferred to other people. One has to live them for oneself. I have some affinity with Kailash. Lord Shiva, who sits here in perpetual meditation has stored in His throat some poison (may be radioactive), making His throat blue, as a legend says. That is why one of His many names is Nilesh निलेश [epistemologically, Nilesh = *Neel* + *Ishwar* *(Blue* + *Lord)*]. I feel so insignificant in front of Him. I try to capture Him in the frame of my camera. I only hope that I can see Him and remember Him forever. I confirm what I said in my short story *King's Audience*.[5] What one has lived to enrich oneself spiritually cannot be taken away from him. The rest is evanescent.

We have to finally leave to return to our tent. In the tent I enter into a dialogue with our Tibetan guide, Jigme. From his natural standpoint Jigme is a born and devout Buddhist and a natural philosopher. He talks of Buddha's *Nirvana* in the same manner and confidence as Einstein probably talked on relativity. I ask him the fundamental question of philosophy. The question remains, *is it better To Be or Not To Be.* If *Being* is better - why did the great Buddha preach *Nirvana (Not- Being)?* The whole world is aflame with his *Idea*. On the contrary if *Nirvana is better,* how can I ever experience what I experience now as a *Being?* One thing is sure. Once it is admitted that *Being* is better, it is difficult to stop short of God. If we admit that *Not-Being* is better, then the discussion ceases to be. This is the great dilemma. Jigme affirms without reasoning that *Nirvana* is a superior existence. He misses the argument. It is too much for me. I end the discussion by giving him his say and remembering the words of Shakespeare: *It is more matter for a May morning (Twelfth Night).*

I wish Jagdishbhai were also involved in the discussion. He is a gifted philosopher. He supports his arguments with quotations from the Upanishads. His knowledge of Sanskrit bewitches me. To be honest, I am so envious because I know no Sanskrit except the Devanagari script that is common with Hindi. As the knowledge of old Greek and modern German are extremely necessary for the study of Western Philosophy, there can be no Eastern philosophy without Sanskrit. Jagdishbhai reads Sanskrit and interprets the verses of the old scriptures. Being a minor philosopher, he is

---

[5] Printed here at the end of this letter, pp. 61-63.

capable of lecturing on Indian philosophy. He is a firm
believer in the principle of *Non-duality (advaita)*. He affirms
that Indian philosophy is a way of living a concrete, complete
life contrary to Western philosophy that is more of intellectual
gymnastics. Western philosophy has in modern times
indeed turned to minute details of words, their
interpretations and language skills and can be rightfully
called academic exercises. Still, Western philosophers
influence me. Descartes and his theory of *Cogito Ergo Sum*
fascinate me. On the Indian side I am attracted towards the
theory of *Purusha and Prakriti* (theory of *Patanjali* who
was a student of *Nagarjun*). I have no way of reading
Patanjali in the original Sanskrit except in English, German,
French, Hindi or Gujarati translations. I wish I had also learnt
Sanskrit. Jagdishbhai and myself stand on the opposite
banks of the *same Reality*. We have together travelled a long
way to realize the Ultimate Truth, *That* which is Immutable.

The Hindus believe that bathing in the clear waters of
Mansarovar cleans one of all the karmic debts. There is no
greater holy water than Mansarovar. Even the waters of the
holy Ganges fall a little lower in degree in holiness to the
water of Mansarovar. We have travelled so far to Mansarovar
and not taking a bath in the holy water would deprive us of
some mystic effect of holy water on our esoteric lives. We
are conscious that we have not had regular daily baths
during the journey. To dip in Mansarovar would dirty the
clear, divine waters. So we find a solution. Our kitchen
personnel erect a tent about two hundred metres away from
the shore. The holy Mansarovar water is carried to the
kitchen tent in containers and warmed up and we take a
bucket bath in the tent. This way we bathe with the holy
water, not dirty the lake, and quench our desire to be
liberated from all karmic debts. On 9 May we are leaving
Kailash and Mansarovar behind us. It is a million dollar
memory for life and life after. Mansarovar in the backdrop of
Kailash is the crown of our pilgrimage.

It is 10 May. We are proceeding southeast towards Saga.

A View of Mount Everest or Sagarmath
(Photo by Dr. Hemant Mehta)

Another View of Mount Everest or Sagarmath
(Photo by Dr. Hemant Mehta)

On the 11ᵗʰ we drive towards Tingri towards the Everest base camp. We spend the 11ᵗʰ, 12ᵗʰ and 13ᵗʰ in the ambience of the great Everest. The name Everest given to this magnificent mountain is not the original name. It is a gift of British colonialism. In the year 1856 it was so named to honour Sir George Everest who was then in the service of India. Sir Everest never saw or visited the mountain given his name. We *indulge in an orgy of photography* in the words of Stephen Venables. Film after film is loaded and exposed. One hears the shutters of the cameras buzzing constantly. The shutters buzz so often that I feel that a team of maharajas is squeezing the triggers of their rifles to shoot one single Bengal tiger. We photograph Sagarmath in the morning and in the evening light. Hemantbhai remains remote and frames his photos alone as always. Kunjbhai has a wide variety of photos in slides and negative films taken with his different cameras. Mrinalini is always co-operative and helpful in taking my photos against the backdrop of Sagarmath. Jagdishbhai is so engrossed in the gripping beauty that he pays no attention to my offers to take some memory pictures of him. In this mood we walk from there towards the North base camp, to the tents where mountaineers from different countries of the world are ready to conquer Sagarmath.

On the way we visit Rongbuk Monastery and bump into a group of local pilgrims who drink and sprinkle the water of a holy spring that flows between the old monastery and the new one on the side of Everest. These pilgrims are poor, very friendly and colourful. Unfortunately, I have left my camera behind. I request Kunjbhai to take my pictures with some of these pilgrims. Their penury is evident from their clothes.

We meet them again at the Rongbuk Monastery. These solemn pilgrims crowd the terrace of the monastery. They are very kind. Each of them offers to share with us the little food they are having at the terrace. We walk through their

crowd taking a grain from each of them, honouring their
sentiments. We cannot talk to them. We only greet them
with *Taschideli,* a greeting amongst Tibetans. Love binds us
together. Kunjbhai is very busy taking their photographs
with Everest thrusting its head skyward in the background.

I follow Vinodbhai in the cave of the mountain. He
suggests that I see the meditation enclave of the monastery.
He has just been there. A monk offers him coffee. Vinodbhai
is delighted. While Vinodbhai is sipping coffee the monk
takes me to the meditation enclave that is deep down in the
mountain. The monk tells me that Nagarjun came here and
stayed at the monastery. He also meditated in this same
cave. I feel as if I am in Alibaba's cave. No light penetrates
into the depth of the meditation enclave. The Buddhist
monk lights a candle. The burning candle dispels the total
darkness. It is a magic touch. Gold glitters in the light. What
state is this? I ask myself. I am dazzled. I feel as if I am
transferred to another dimension.

I have a strong urge to meditate. For the first time I have
success in meditation. This success is the very hub of my
pilgrimage. I realise that I am not simply my body. No
materialist can from this moment render arguments and
persuade me otherwise. Without this magnificent experience I would have been disillusioned. My enthusiastic efforts
to make such a long journey would have been in vain. I
would ask myself if meditation has any value at all. Now my
experience assures me that meditation is the crown of all
activities of a man during his life. It is a conscious process
to inward progress.

I do not notice any loud breathing even though there is
little or no air. I forget my bodily existence. I see myself
carried away in a trance. I am far away from all activity. I am
bathing and drenched in the all white Mansarovar. The air is
fragrant with the scent of flowers. It is not cold. I do not feel
the touch of ice water. I experience as if I am dipping and
soaking in pure white light. I feel as if I am a witness to a

new cosmic creation around me. The source of this creation is Kailash in front of me. On top of Kailash there is a white temple with a beautiful long staircase in white marble. I see Shiva sitting in front of the temple, serene and sovereign in perpetual meditation. He is beauty, bliss and benevolence all at once. Some sort of mysterious divine music (not a bhajan) is all persistent and entirely around me. Time has declined to be. Still, everything is in a flux of creation. At one moment I think I have always been here. There is no past, present or future. It is a feeling of perpetuity at one moment, at one bang. Countless white lilies are floating in the air. I am enveloped in total perfection. No desires rush. Mind is in absolute peace. How can my moderate language express the beauty of this heavenly ambience? How can my inadequate mortal speech express the splendour of an esoteric world?

I try to climb the white marble stairs. I want to reach Shiva in front of the temple. I hear a voice asking me repeatedly, *do you know yourself?* I am confused. I don't know myself. Hence I ask myself, *do I know myself?* I am unable to form a candid reply. One complaint I have against myself. At such moments, I am always dumbfounded and unable to express myself in words. At this moment I wish I had confidently said, *yes, I know who I am.* But alas, words fail me more than ever. Being in a state of perplexity, not knowing the answer, I come down to myself, in my body seated in the lighted cave. I feel my body is very heavy. My spirit is light with innate joy.

For a moment I don't recognise the room. Sitting before me is the Buddhist monk and not Shiva. I now capture what has happened. Never shall I forget the impact of this experience. I leave the meditation room in a reflective frame of mind. I wish I could stay longer meditating. In fact I feel I should stay here at this monastery forever. The impact of spiritual force and experience remains with me while I descend the hill of the monastery. All the time I wonder if this is really the fulfilment of my wish for vision of Shiva, made as the shooting star fell down during the night of 26 April. I get a strong inner confirmation.

In this mode I walk further to the foot of Everest. Somehow even being so near to Everest, I now feel very detached from it. I feel disinterested. At the camp at the foot of Everest, the Spanish, the Korean and the Japanese have set out to climb the Everest peak. It's a race as to who is going to conquer the peak first this season. I am not in the race. Thank God. I feel as if I am living in Eternity. I am saturated with a million impressions of travel. This is the last phase of our pilgrimage.

Next day, on 14 May, we are on our way to Nepal with the intention of staying two nights at Dhulikhel. It is our last day in Tibet. All the way, Kunjbhai takes a lot of photos, some memory snaps. I am now tired of photography. I show a desire to meet a Yeti. There is such a big controversy regarding the existence of yetis. A Tibetan (not a part of our team) tells me a story that I find fascinating. He tells me that Yetis exist on the higher regions of the *Sagarmath* (Everest). In the ancient days (time unknown) there was a big colony of them. Once during an organised feast they drank a lot of *chiang* (Tibetan alcohol) and in intoxication battled with pointed weapons. The feast ended with the death of all the Yetis. Only one Yeti family, which decided not to take part in the festival but watch it from a distance survived. The family moved to the higher regions of the mountains and avoid men whom they do not trust. They still live in a very close group and over time how big this family has grown cannot be estimated. Their domain is Everest and they know every centimetre of Everest. They hide from all men. This story appeals to me.

In contrast to this saga, Harishbhai and Dorje, our Nepalese companion, tell me that Yetis *do not exist*. These *bristly savage snowmen,* they say, are a myth. I have always wondered how a myth originates *without any foundation*. How can it be sustained so long? I also don't know why

Reinhold Messner, the famous Austrian mountaineer, said that yetis are a reality and he was face to face with a yeti. He made this bold disclosure at a press conference. The cultivated world pooh-poohed at him, making him sound like a nincompoop. In Reinhold's German book *Legende Und Wirklichkeit*[6] (publishers *Fischer Verlag*), I read with much curiosity that he allocates a whole chapter to his meeting with a Yeti. He titles it, *Wie ich zum Yeti kam* (how I came to a Yeti). I find his treatise fascinating. I believe in people, in what they say and their feelings and their faith. I believe in the Tibetan who narrated the story of the Yeti's existence and in Reinhold who knew what he was talking about. To me these people are not insane. Still, at this stage I don't *know* the truth at first hand. This mystery will probably remain curtained in my lifetime. I give a close and long look at Everest during the last hour at the base camp. I wonder how many more mysteries are still enveloped in this majestic mountain. The last days at Everest base camp are very picturesque.

We drive towards the Nepal border. The route to Naylam through the mountain range is the most colourful part of our travel. I watch the stages of the return journey as they pass very swiftly before my eyes. At Naylam we are to stay one night. Naylam, though beautifully situated in the hills, has no hotel to attract us. There is a hotel on the main street but it has toilets and showers across the street. Each one of us is tired and we yearn for more luxury. We change our plan and abruptly decide to drive further. We drive towards Zhangmu. Zhangmu is a border town and has a good hotel. There are road repairs and entering the hilly Zhangmu requires more than two hours. We stay at Zhangmu Government hotel. At the hotel there is a surprise dinner. Jagdishbhai invites all of us for a grand dinner at the hotel restaurant. After an elaborate dinner, luscious and hot, set in style *a la art*

---

[6] Legend And Reality.

Tibetan, a luxury *par excellence,* we stand up and drink *le santé* of Urvashiben whose birthday we celebrate in her absence with great éclat. I especially relish a glass of sparkling wine. It is *aussi la fête pour l'anniversaire de Monsieur et Madame* Jagdish Trivedi. This is an unforgettable, positive memory.

Next morning we walk to the border. The kitchen's personnel involve themselves in the customs inspection formalities. It is thrilling to walk between two different nations. It is a long walk. We walk over the bridge in the lush green no man's land. Suddenly all nature is a festival of spring. It is clothed in fresh green. Branches with vibrant green leaves that tower above, nestling chirping birds that trumpet a song in chorus attract our attention. Streams of water are falling loudly on both sides of the valley. The trees are adorned with flowers. The roads are lined with fragrant blooms. It is a pleasure to see a red rose in full bloom. It is now an embodiment of divine love. The entire world is filled with His embrace for all is joy, colours, blooms, ardent rays and perfumed breeze. I also see a peacock proudly spreading its magnificently designed feathers in the spray of the falling water. I feel as if the bliss world of the Christians, the jannat of Koran or the vaikunth of the Vaishnavas is manifested on earth. What a blessing I am alive. There are grand rows of small Nepalese shops on both sides. The shops have wonderful and colourful textiles and things with art designs on display. The walk is very pleasant. The valley grows narrower. The faces and costumes also change. A few Nepalese women are attired in Punjabi dresses. The sight makes us feel that we are getting nearer home.

On the Nepalese side of the border a minibus is waiting for us that will take us to *Dhulikhel,* a holiday resort in Nepal. We say goodbye to Jigme and all the members of the Tibetan team. They return to Lhasa leaving us here. We were a family for five weeks. It is an emotional parting. We hug each other and promise to write as often as possible. We

walk further down the no man's land. We are filled with
gentle emotions. These emotions are a weird but wonderful
mixture of sorrow and joy. We are completing our most
memorable pilgrimage that can never be repeated in the
same constellation. We are completing a rare *rendezvous* of
our life. We are leaving behind a childhood dream that has
just been realized. We are saying *au revoir* to the love and
amity of a holy land. We are leaving behind turquoise lakes
mirroring the magical ambience of lofty colorful hills. We are
bidding farewell to majestic mountains united with Gods.
We are saying bye to bubbling virgin rivers that give life to
millions. We are also physically saying *adieu* to Shiva and
the holy Mansarovar. They gave me so much of love and
vision. Their memories will lure me for the rest of my life.
The pilgrimage is over with a new vision, a new promise of
love for life and a new set of values defined. For all these,
I regret it is ending. I say aloud *auf wiedersehen* in German
meaning I wish to *see you again.* To say goodbye to
something you hold so dear is the gloomy side of the
medallion. On the merrier side, I am happy that I am going
to the home soon sharing these experiences with my family.
I have such a lot to tell them. It is so thrilling to share these
unique experiences. I feel my sons Niraj and Suraj will want
to come here. They will want to share my joy, my values. It
is surely a positive end for a new beginning.

In this mood I cross the bridge, never knowing that a
disaster waits only a breath away. To describe it here is
essential except no words can express its shock. A road
repair and construction is the cause of intense rock blasting.
This compels us to descend a steep slope. There is no
alternative offered. Though at some stage we think it is
unwise to walk down. We underestimate its complexity. It is
dangerous. Once we begin to descend there is no return.
With great relief we manage to reach the foot of the hill.
Some of us descend with the help of Gurkhas who protect
our security in return for a small gift of cash. Our minds are

in despair for the hazardous descent. Once at the foot of the
hill we are tired and sitting down at the base of the hill. We
are in a pensive mood. An inner voice tells us to move away
from the spot. May be some Himalayan God, pleased with
our pilgrimage, as an unexpected boon, whispers in our
hearts and motivates us to move away from that place to a
safer place. We move away from that place.

A negative experience follows. Ten minutes later, at that
very same spot, big and heavy rocks slide down. They
would have smashed us to dust instantly. This accident
shakes all of us at the border crossing the Friendship Bridge
between Tibet and Nepal. It could have miserably killed one
or all of us. My mind needlessly occupies itself with the
other alternative that is forever, thank god, unknown. What
if......Who would have even recognised our bodies in the
debris of tumbling rocks and smashed earth. During the
approximately three thousand kilometres of our travelling,
this is the only moment when we come only an inch away
from death. To think of it, this moment is like a dark
nightmare. Only a divine angel saves our lives.

Devastated, we board the waiting cars to register ourselves at the Nepalese immigration office. I note down this
incident elaborately in my diary. I make regular notes in my
diary and record everything I experience. At a later stage I
shall contemplate on them. This letter will be posted from
the first available post office. We spend the night of the 15th
at Dhulikhel. I wonder if it is possible to post it in Dhulikhel.
Surely, it may be possible in Kathmandu. If there is a depot
where I am able to put these words on a diskette and print
it out, I shall be delighted. Otherwise I will post a photocopy
of my hand-written letter. In that case I sincerely wish that
you are able to decipher my hieroglyphs. When I reread my
notes, I ponder on myself. Once the journey is over and I am
back in my apartment in Vienna, how much will this small
period of time but large in experience really add to me? I
know that I have enriched myself spiritually. On returning to

the point of beginning, I know it will change my inner life, a thing that won't show outwardly. For the world, for everyone who knows me, for you, I will remain exactly as I was before. Only I know inwardly that I will never be the same. I am aware of one thing that how *cœur de la matière* (heart of the matter) influence *le milieu divin* (the divine setting) with each experience we make. Tomorrow is 17 May. I am ready to fly back to Vienna. I will fly miles away from Tibet. Still I know for certain that I can never part from Tibet. Tibet will never leave me, neither Kailash nor Mansarovar. From now on they are an undying part of my body, life and soul. They should remain so.

I think of you during my whole meditation and escapade in the Himalayas and send my love. I think of you while I visit the various monasteries and temples. You are included in my prayers and meditation. We send our kindest regards.

Yours sincerely,

Nilesh

WE:
Mr. Vinod Budhdeo   Dr. Hemant Mehta
Jigme, Dorje   Mr. Harish Kapadia
Dr. (Mrs.) Mrinalini Mehta   Dawa, Lee, Pasang
Mr. Kunj Trivedi   Nilesh Nathwani
La, Motilal, Chandra   Mr. Jagdish Trivedi
and many more.

A re-reading of this diary convinces me that before I set out to print it, though with great diffidence, I should let others of my team read it. I want my readers to know that the views expressed here are solely mine. They express conclusions reached by the stressful and careful process known as thinking. Whenever some new thinking is presented,

others should be vigilant to confirm or refute it.[7] *With this
conviction I am sending this diary to the first six members
of our expedition listed above. They have lived with me
during the Kailash-Mansarovar expedition. They may sug-
gest some alterations that I may or may not like to include.
For sure I cannot expect them to sanction all my views. It is
possible that some readers find a few concepts difficult to
accept. I only wish that these readers viewed things with the
eye of my "I". With this plea and the following lines from
Shelly, I present my diary:*

> *I can give not what men call love*
> *But will thou accept not*
> *The worship the heart lifts above*
> *And the Heavens reject not*

NILESH DWARKADAS NATHWANI

---

[7] If you have something to say about this book, kindly e-mail the author
directly:
E-mail: **nilesh.nathwani@vienna.at**

EPILOGUE

For four major religions of the world, i.e. for Tibetan Buddhism, Jainism, Bompo (a religion prior to Buddhism in Tibet) and Hinduism, Mount Kailash is the spot of utmost reverence and importance.

For the Buddhists, Kailash is the centre point of the universe. Many Tibetan Buddhist thinkers and spiritual giants engaged in long meditations to realise Nirvana at the foot of Kailash. So many monasteries around Kailash and Mansarovar bear witness to this living truth even today. The tale of the philosopher-king, Milarepa, who ascended the glowing lighted peak of Kailash and attained the highest spiritual height, is a marvel still living in the hearts of Tibetan Buddhists. Padmasambhava, who brought Buddhism to Tibet, also spent the last years of his life in deep meditation and probably attained Nirvana here. For some schools of Buddhism, *this centre of the world* is the only powerful place to realise Nirvana, as Buddha's force is ever present here.

For the Jains, Kailash is the Mount Ashtapada and is a place of pilgrimage. It is at the foot of Ashtapada, that Adinath Rishabhdev, one of their first prophets, and some other gurus achieved enlightenment.

For the Bompo followers, Kailash is the nine-faced Swastika Mountain and is constantly emanating great power. The number nine is also a spiritual number that helps to invoke the latent influence and spiritual power of an individual. The followers of this concept walk around Kailash in an anticlockwise course to invoke the maximum mystic powers of Nature.

For the Hindus, Kailash is the Sumeru Parvat, the spiritual centre of the world around which all the earthly powers revolve. Kailash-Mansarovar is the abode of Lord Shiva, Parvati (his female consort) and their two sons, Ganesh (the elephant-headed child) and Subrahmanya. Adored and worshipped all over India, they are very important and

remain as living deities for their worshippers. Most of the
devoted Hindus who go there attempt to make a "parikrama"
(or circumambulation) of both Kailash and Mansarovar.
Mansarovar, as the name suggests, is the lake created by
Brahma the Creator out of his mind (manas). It is generally
known that aquatic life is the first concrete life form in the
process of evolution. Perhaps, Brahma also created the first
life at Mansarovar. Matsya, the fish incarnation of Vishnu,
was also born at Mansarovar, as narrated in Hindu mythology.
The geographical position of the sweet water lake is really
celestial. The settings of light and water are in perfect blend
here. The reflections of Kailash and Mount Gurla Mandata
on Mansarovar in the evening hours, when the golden
slanting rays of the sun penetrate through the pure, unpolluted
air, are a sight to wonder. When Mansarovar, Kailash and
Gurla Mandata are all lit up in the afterglow of the dusk, it
is as if a light show is being displayed in the sky. For the
devotees, this is a unique experience of being one with the
celestial power on an earthly plane.

A Hindu is made to understand the grand cosmic design,
the origin of the universe and man's place in it through
simple stories told in the mythological tales. Mythology is an
ideal medium for theoretical and practical education.
Mythological stories easily elucidate the origin of the world,
its complexities and the subtle worlds around us. Reason
often fails to explain these. These stories are narrated again
and again as bedtime stories or small plays at festival time.
Various festivals celebrated on religions occasions in India
constantly enrich the life of Hindus. Thousands of such
stories exist. As per these stories, Lord Shiva and many other
Gods live at Kailash-Mansarovar, making it glorious and
divine. These stories remain vivid in the minds of the
worshippers. Furthermore, some holy men of India have
narrated stories about their authentic and personal encounter
with Lord Shiva at Kailash-Mansarovar. These holy men,
who work as mediators between men and Gods, claim that

they attained their highest spiritual realisation at Kailash or
Mansarovar. Spiritual salvation and darshan (direct encounter)
of God attracts the devout Hindu very much and remains the
core of his life mission. He wants to see God face to face
during his lifetime. Day after day he endeavours to be in
unison with God. He talks to Him, plays with Him, dreams
of Him. I also dreamt of Him. For the devout Hindu, the Lord
and His multiple personalities are very real and approachable.
That Gods can be easily approached at Kailash-Mansarovar
is profoundly engraved in their minds. Even for me, the
striving and underpinning motivation to go as far as Kailash-
Mansarovar was to achieve this realisation—to see God face
to face and talk with Him. This notion predominantly rules
the minds of all the ardent seekers of the Ultimate Reality.
Therefore, Kailash-Mansarovar is considered to be the most
important of all the pilgrimages one can make during one's
lifetime to attain spiritual salvation.

When one sees Kailash from near and particularly from
the middle point of the base of the south face (when coming
from the Indian side, the south face is the first vision of
Kailash), one cannot fail to see a massive Shiva figure sitting
in perpetual meditation at his permanent abode with the
snow flakes flying in the air. The contour of Kailash composes
this figure. It is like seeing a lion or a castle in the contour
of a low-hanging white cloud. He sits there real and mighty.
Lord Shiva has the contradictory attributes of being the
destroyer and restorer of the Universe, a perfect blend of
opposites. Hence, He is the supreme deity. The numerous
stories of the unique and mighty Lord Shiva living at Kailash,
as narrated in the *Shiva Purana,* fascinate Hindus for all time.

Though Lord Shiva is a cosmic power, it is fascinating
how artists normally depict him. Ash coloured, Lord Shiva is
shown bare or half naked, wearing only a loincloth, His
neck is blue from holding and storing the poison thrown up
during the churning of the cosmic ocean. Mythology recounts
that He was the only Lord who could store this poison in
suspension (between His mouth and abdomen), a poison so

deadly that it threatened to destroy mankind forever. His
hair is arranged in a coil of matted, curly locks adorned with
a crescent moon dripping the nectar of eternal life and the
river Ganges trickling through His hair. On His forehead, He
has a third eye concentrating on the occult inner micro-
universe. His third eye, if opened and focused outwards, is
capable of burning and destroying the material world. He
wears a serpent around His neck (it is interesting to note
here that a Tibetan told me that the most rare snakes, not to
be seen anywhere else in the world, inhabit the caves of
Kailash). It is a known fact that snake venom or Lachesis, is
a very useful medicine. Kailash is also home to numerous
herbal medicines. That is why one of Lord Shiva's many
names is also Vaidyanath or Lord of Healers. Some of His
other names are Naageshwar (Lord of Serpents), Dakshina
Murti (Great Teacher), Natraj (King of Dance), Pashupati
(Lord of animals) and many more. Often His four hands are
shown carrying a trident and a damaru (a small drum), a
tongue of fire and an open hand in a gesture of Divine grace
flowing from above (also indicating "do not be afraid"). Now
let us briefly examine some of these aspects and draw
parallels. The serpent is a symbol of medicine. Even in
chemists' shops it is exposed as an emblem. The drum
symbolises the rhythm of the universe and also characterises
the Big Bang Theory. The tongue of flame on the left hand
means that the transcendental nature of the universe is
hidden behind the aspirations of men. The open palm of the
right hand is a gesture of grace and is to remind us that grace
is constantly flowing from above and there is no need for us
to fear the destruction which is inevitable. These meanings,
as I have interpreted, here, are derived from whatever little I
have read and are not absolute. Fantasy has no limits. There is
no end to the lengths one can go on in interpreting the crescent
moon, the water, the serpent, the bareness of the Lord, the third
eye, the blue neck, His dark complexion, etc., etc.

My aim is not to enter into any dialectical controversies
over the Holy Mountain. Kailash is beautiful par excellence.

What Ralph W. Emerson said of beauty can be very well said of God also. He said, *though we travel the world over to find the beautiful, we must carry it with us or we will find it not.* The pilgrims are in search of what is already inside them. They are inspired to continue their pilgrimage along the mythological path, seeing Gods in the heavenly abode of Shiva. It may win them celestial awards, though we are blind to such rewards in present life. Let it be so. To ignore and judge the accounts of many saints and regard Kailash as an ordinary mountain is a great loss for all those sceptical visitors who want to go there simply for trekking. To remain suspicious of religion may affirm that one is rational, intelligent and different from the masses. This may help feed one's ego. Or it may be that one is turning a blind eye to the real inner enemies living within us in the forms of egoism, arrogance, complexes or even fear—fear of facing a mighty power. For any rational being, to accept Kailash as the abode of the Lord, is the right approach. The immediate awards are bountiful and remind us of our duty towards Nature. Nature is a sufficient boon to feel Heaven or Bliss or Swarga or Jannat as a concrete experience of reality right in front of us. It is proper to accept that a mighty power, that is The Law of Nature, exists. This has the power of changing the destiny of an individual, a nation or the entire world. This becomes very evident when one sees Lord Shiva sitting at Kailash in deep meditation and peace. Peace will flow into us if we allow it to penetrate by way of meditation. In this thermonuclear age, if civilisation takes this ideal as a pillar, we will not disintegrate into a myth after a nuclear war. We can shrug off a great deal of destruction and continue enjoying the luxuries of life by accepting the Laws of Nature. In my opinion it is actually rewarding to be full of devotion. I personally enjoyed being a pilgrim in full faith. At times even I had to use the strength of my will to shut off my rational mind to see Him sitting there. I admit that I did not succeed every time. For those lapses, Benevolent Lord Shiva, I bow down to You and beg for forgiveness.

Appendices

Appendix A

APROPOS

The Himalayan Mountains act as a shield protecting India from the bitter cold winds. Very cold winds blow in Tibet throughout the year. So one has to be very careful in selecting the time of visit and lucky to get right weather conditions while visiting Kailash-Mansarovar. *The best time for visiting is from mid-May to the end of June.* During this time of the year, the weather is normally dependable and visibility remains crystal clear. The air warms up when the sun shines while the nights are inevitably freezing.

There is a direct route from the Indian side crossing the border at Lipu Lekh Pass. The pilgrimage is organized by the Uttar Pradesh State Government and is a package deal that covers all expenses including transport. It provides vegetarian food. The primary requirement of the tour is that the traveller possesses the medical fitness certificate test. It is indeed a hard journey that involves trekking at 4700 meters above sea level. The parikrama around Kailash is about 52 km. and the parikrama around Mansarovar is around 75 km. Anyone interested in this package deal should apply to Ministry of External Affairs. Please take note that every year only 200 pilgrims are selected amongst thousands of applicants. Talking to some pilgrims who have done this pilgrimage, I found out that the trip to Kailash-Mansarovar is so tempting that some pilgrims repeat it every year under a different name. The cost of such a pilgrimage comes to approximately Indian Rupees 30,000, and the duration of the trip is 32 days starting from Delhi. One should be prepared to sleep in huge tents. Toilet facilities are minimal. More information can be collected from Kumaon Mandal Vikas Nigam (KMVN) and the state travel information services of Uttar Pradesh who also arrange for the visas to visit Tibet. There are many

other private organized tours offered by various travel agents
in India. The tours are organized over Kathmandu and visas
are obtained from the Chinese Consulate at Kathmandu. It is
reassuring to note that such tours are less bureaucratic while
they cost a little more than Indian Rupees 45,000. The route
offered is the south motorway over the Nepal-China
Friendship Bridge that takes you first to Mansarovar and
then to Kailash.

Our trip started from Kathmandu. The total cost was
about Indian Rupees 3,50,000 per person. This included my
air fare from Vienna to Kathmandu and return. It was
privately organized by Himalaya Expeditions, P.O. Box 105,
(e-mail *himalaya@mos.com.np*) Kathmandu, Nepal. They
also arranged for our visas. We arrived in Kathmandu on
15th April, 2000 and stayed overnight at Hotel Vaishali
(e-mail *vaishali@vishnu.ccsl.com.np*) a really luxurious hotel
for a pilgrim. After three days in Nepal we flew to Lhasa, Tibet
with Chinese National Airways. Lhasa has a very posh hotel
—Lhasa Hotel, Minzu Lu, Lhasa, Tibet, Republic of China
(Phones: 0086 0891 683 22 21 • Fax: 0086 0891 683 57 96).
From Lhasa our group started in two Land cruisers and one
truck. So began our journey to Kailash Mansarovar.

Only at Gyantse and Shigaste, we lived at luxurious
government hotels. After Shigatse we took the Northern
motorway living in tents and local Chinese guesthouses. We
paid about Rupees 200, per bed per night at local
guesthouses. The bed sheets were far from being white,
unwashed and smelt of yak butter. We used our sleeping
bags over the beds. I will give our route in short form.
Lhasa-Gyantse-Shigaste-Lhatse-Sang Sang-Tsuoqing-Geze-
Gegyi-Shiquane (Ali)-Purang-Trethapuri-Darchen-Mansarovar.
From Mansarovar taking the Southern motorway towards
Everest we passed by Nagri Korsum, Porang, Old Tingri,
and Rongbuk Monastery. We stayed two nights at the
Everest base camp. Travelling further towards Nepal we
stayed at Zhangmu and crossing the Nepal-China Friendship
Bridge returned to Kathmandu over Dhulikhel.

It is important to note that for taking photographs and movies in the interior of the monasteries, one is required to pay charges that differ from monastery to monastery. At times these could be exorbitant. One cannot buy quality photographic material in Tibet except in Lhasa. So one is advised to carry enough of it with oneself. It is best to carry professional material as photography in the bright sunlight of Tibet is a delight.

One should be prepared to accept loss of appetite, fatigue, headache, nausea, dizziness, palpitations, sleeplessness, shortness of breath as normal as these are common symptoms of acute mountain sickness. One should still seek medical advice. Once one is on such a high altitude, avoid rapid movements and even talking. Drinking a lot of water helps to minimise these sicknesses. One pays a high price for such an adventure and so one must be mentally prepared to accept a lot of inconvenience. Despite all the inconveniences, I am of the opinion that there is no journey like Kailash-Mansarovar. It is certainly a unique experience. If there are heavenly abodes on earth, Kailash-Mansarovar is to be treasured as one that is the most celestial.

Appendix B

KING'S AUDIENCE
(A short story based on a Hindi story)

Once upon a time there was a man, a very robust man, clever and intelligent. He decided to meet the King face to face. Rather, a difficult wish to realise for a commoner. Clever he was he jumped over the palace wall into the Royal Garden. Looking right and left, he lost his orientation. Which way to turn? He turned in one direction and there was a grand mansion with a lovely aroma. He entered the mansion and found that a lovely table was laid out with a great variety of luscious food, all hot and ready. There was no one there and he was hungry. So he helped himself and ate until he could eat no more. *What a delicious treat, I would have been a fool if I had not eaten.* Soon, he heard some music. He turned to the mansion from which this divine melodious music spouted. He came to the ladies' chambers. There was a ballet going on and everyone was engrossed. He sat down and enjoyed the music and dance. To his left was a golden mug with wine. He drank the wine and pocketed the mug of massive gold. Nobody noticed.

Now it is time to meet the King. He turned away unnoticed and went into another direction. He came across a pool with cool waters. He said to himself. *I can't go to the King so unattractive.* So he jumped into the cool waters, cleaned himself, perfumed himself and wore a set of new garments, all readily available.

Meanwhile, the sun had set and the western sky was all lit in the afterglow of the dusk as if an *Aarti (a religious worship)* was performed in the heavenly chambers. He thought *it is so beautiful that I may pause for a while to register the glory of the heavenly sky in kingly style.* Soon the darkness appeared. He got flurried and jumped the high wall and returned home, amused and without seeing the King.

His wife was very happy with the golden mug and congratulated him on adding a fortune to the family assets.

There was another man, his friend, a simple, burly man who was gifted with a modicum of humility, sound wisdom and adamant determination. He also decided to meet the King. He told his wife. She said, *though it is not easy to have his audience, it is possible if you remain strong and targeted.* She said, *do not come back home without your mission fulfilled. I will cook and we will have a meal together.* He went straight to the gatekeeper and asked for an interview with the King. The gatekeeper took him to the King's secretary. The secretary said that he has to inform the Sovereign that his subject wants to see him but this will take time. Meanwhile he can enjoy the Royal hospitality and enjoy a snack and a cold drink. *No,* said the man, *I have already eaten, but will wait here while you inform the King.*

The secretary disappeared and came back at lunch time. The man was still waiting. *How about a nice lunch, while you are waiting. No sir, that might put me to sleep and when the King is ready, I may not be alert. The thought of food is at present far away from my mind while what all I am really worried about is if you have indeed informed the King about my presence here or not. Without seeing him I will not budge from this place.* The secretary was taken aback and thought *this man is adamant.* Meanwhile, it was dusk and the western sky was at its best with its play of myriad colours. The day that was dying but still wanted to live - exhibited its grandeur grand. The secretary told him if he wanted to come again, another time, as it was getting late and he may enjoy the sunset from the royal garden. *No,* he said in settled tenacity. The secretary went inside and informed the King and took the man inside for an audience. He had the sight of the King and performed to him a grand kow-tow, kow-tow in the oriental style. Thereafter he was escorted through the Royal Garden with dignity and passing the main Gate he came back home directly. He was grateful to his wife for the guidance she gave him. He was happy that his mission was fulfilled. He would often recall and narrate his encounter with the King to his family and friends and go in ecstasy. He repeatedly said that what one has lived to enrich oneself spiritually cannot be taken away from him. The rest is evanescent. One should always aim to live to one's highest possibilities.

PARABLE

King – God   Wife - Shakti (power)
Man – Seeker   Secretary - Guru (spiritual mediator)
Royal garden - material world.

Appendix C

LIST OF THE ITEMS TO BE CARRIED[8]

1. Photographs of Grand Parents, Parents, and family members with whom you love to share this Yatra.
2. Wide brimmed hat of cloth/felt with chinstrap.
3. Balaclava/monkey woollen cap.
4. Woollen scarf.
5. Sleeve tee shirts as underwear (maximum four).
6. Cotton underwear (maximum four).
7. Flannel shirts (maximum two).
8. Sleeveless pullover or fleece jacket.
9. Long sleeve thick pullover (one).
10. Coloured trousers with 4 pockets (maximum two including the one on body).
11. Shorts (one).
12. Woollen and acryl socks (four)
13. Long johns (two)
14. Ski jacket.
15. Windbreaker jacket.
16. Woollen gloves /ski gloves.
17. Towel.
18. Napkin.
19. Handkerchief.
20. Mountain shoes.
21. Trainers.
22. Warm slippers.
23. Folding umbrella/raincoat.
24. Air pillow
25. Large carry bag with liner.
26. Swimming costume.
27. Rug sack.

---

[8] This list is an extension of the list provided by Mr. Harish Kapadia.

28. Sleeping bag suitable for temperatures of *minus 20°C.*
29. Walking stick.
30. Drinking water bottle (metal).
31. Hot water bottle.
32. Thermos flask.
33. Sunglasses.
34. Extra pair of spectacles.
35. Watch.
36. Alarm clock.
37. Torch with extra bulb and batteries.
38. Penknife.
39. Diary/notice book.
40. Envelopes and paper.
41. Ball pens.
42. Sewing kit with needles, thread and buttons.
43. First Aid set including painkillers, antibiotics, calendula, arnica and arsenic alb D^{200} etc.
44. Sun protection cream.
45. Lip balm.
46. Camera with wide angle and tele optics.
47. Camera films. (At least 2 with higher sensitivity, say 800 ASA)
48. Binoculars.
49. Nail cutter.
50. Comb.
51. Hair cream.
52. Shaving set.
53. Tooth brush.
54. Toilet paper rolls/ Wet wipes
55. Tooth paste
56. Soap.
57. Washing powder.

BIBLIOGRAPHY

Tibet—Maria Antonia Sironi Deimberger, Kurt Deimberger. Karl Müller Verlag.

Seven Years in Tibet—Heinrich Harrer. Econo-Clad Books.

Everest Kangshung Face—Stephen Venables. Hodder and Stoughton.

Sumeru Parvat—Swami Bikash Giri. Kailash Asram, U.P. India.

Collected Poems—Sri Aurobindo. Sri Aurobindo Ashram, Pondicherry.

Savitri—Sri Aurobindo. Sri Aurobindo Ashram, Pondicherry.

The Message Of the Gita As Interpreted by Sri Aurobindo— Anilbaran Roy.Sri Aurobindo Ashram, Pondicherry.

Die Bhagavadgita—S. Radhakrishnan. Holle Verlag, Baden-Baden, Germany.

Divina Commedia-Paradiso—Dante Alighieri. Tascabili Economici Newton, Roma

Talks On Poetry—Amal Kiran. Sri Aurobindo International Centre of Education, Pondicherry.

Heiligesten Berg der Welt—Herbert Tichy. Zum Buchgemeinschaft Donauland/Wien

Legende Und Wirklichkeit—Reinhold Messner. Fischer Verlag.

A Journey to Tibet—Dr. Hemant Mehta, FRCS; FRPS. An article from Foto Art, Spring 2001, Newsletter of the Royal Photographic Society Colour Group, Great Britain.

Encyclopaedia Britannica—Helen Hemingway Benton, Publisher, edition 1977.

Total Kailash—Harish Kapadia. An unpublished report.

Various Tourist Guides on Tibet—Available in English, German and French.

THE HINDU MIND (Fundamentals of Hindu Religion and Philosophy for All Ages)—*Bansi Pandit*

Hinduism is the oldest surviving religion in the world. The religious and philosophical literature of Hinduism is vast, diverse and covers thousands of years of accumulated spiritual experiences of Hindu Saints and Seers. This book presents the fundamentals of Hindu religion and philosophical thought in a logical and straightforward manner. The purpose being, to create a strong base for further study of Hinduism.

ISBN: 81-7822-007-5

THE BOOK OF BUDDHAS (Ritual Symbolism used on Buddhist Statuary and Ritual Objects)—*Eva Rudy Jansen*

This book explores the symbolism of the ritual objects that are used on statues and paintings, as well as explaining the ritual meaning of the objects associated with Buddhism. This book serves as an introduction for Western students. Though is not a comprehensive and exhausting study, but provides an introduction to Buddhism itself, as well as a generous survey of the most common figures and symbols.

ISBN: 81-7822-055-5

THE BOOK OF HINDU IMAGERY (Gods and their Symbols)
—*Eva Rudy Jansen*

Hinduism is more than a religion; it is a way of life that has developed over approximately 5 millennia. Its rich and multicultured history, has made the structure of its mythical and philosophical principles into a highly differentiated maze, of which total knowledge is a practical impossibility. Though volume does not offer a complete survey of the meaning of Hinduism, but it does provide an extensive compilation of important deities and their divine manifestations, to make modern students understand the significance of the Hindu pantheon.

ISBN: 81-7822-056-3

TANTRA WITHOUT TEARS—*Christopher S. Hyatt* and *S. Jason Black*

This book gives you the understanding and ability to use certain symbols, sounds and images that you will find in more conventional and classical texts. In other words, as well as an instructional text, it is also a jumping off point for those who wish to pursue the original Eastern material at another time. This book tells one how to achieve and utilize power to meet one's own needs and suit one's own ends. It is not about common notions of harmony or agels or anything like that. It is not sweet-and-light and is full of real-world experiences which reflect the workings of Tantric philosophy and practice.

ISBN: 81-7822-027-x